REPORTERS at WAR

ALICE FLEMING

This book pays a well-deserved tribute to the courageous newspaper correspondents who go to the front lines of battle and write honestly of the brilliance, the bravery, the brutality, and the blunders that make up the many faces of war.

Beginning with William Howard Russell, the Englishman who covered the infamous Charge of the Light Brigade during the Crimean War, the author recounts the adventurous careers of ten great reporters, including Januarius Aloysius MacGahan, known as the "Cossack correspondent;" Winston Churchill, who first became famous for his daring escape from his South African captors during the Boer War;

Continued on the back flap

REPORTERS
AT
WAR

REPORTERS
AT
WAR

by Alice Fleming

COWLES BOOK COMPANY, INC.
NEW YORK

Contents

Preface

It has been more than a hundred years since a newspaper editor first sent a reporter off to war. Since then, thousands of men—and an occasional woman—have been present on history's too numerous battlefields. These unarmed, and often unsung, correspondents have brought anxious nations the good news—or bad—of their armies' actions. They have written about the many faces of war—the brilliance and the bravery, the brutality and the blunders.

A good correspondent needs two qualities—the courage to go into battle and the honesty to report it. The people in this book had both. Hopefully, their stories will give the reader some idea of what it means to be a reporter at war.

1

William Howard Russell

On a quiet February evening in 1854, a thirty-four-year-old reporter named William Howard Russell was busy in the office of the London *Times*. Suddenly a messenger appeared at his desk. The newspaper's editor, John T. Delane, wanted to see Russell at once.

Expecting no more than a routine assignment, the genial black-haired young journalist strolled into his editor's office and was greeted with the astonishing news that a British expeditionary force was about to embark for the Mediterranean. England was on the verge of going to war against Russia and Delane wanted Russell to cover the story.

If his employee had any objections to the plan, John T. Delane didn't wait to hear them. He had already asked Lord Hardinge, the commander in chief of the British army, to procure an order for Russell's passage from Southampton with the Coldstream Guards.

"You will be back at Easter, depend on it," Delane assured him, "and you will have a pleasant trip."

Delane was wrong on both counts. England officially entered the Crimean War in March and two Easters passed before William Howard Russell returned to London. Nor by any stretch of the imagination could his trip be described as pleasant. At one point he wrote home that he was living in a "pigstye without chair, table, stool or window glass and an old hag of sixty to attend to me who doesn't understand a word I say." Nevertheless, Russell's unexpected expedition to the Crimea won him the distinction of being the first newspaper reporter in history to accompany an army into battle.

A tall, good-natured Irishman, the pioneer war correspondent was born at Lily Vale on the outskirts of Dublin on March 28, 1820. "There," he wrote in his memoirs, "my mother's father, Captain John, or, as he was generally called, Jack, Kelly had a small property and a big untidy house where he held revels as master of the Tallaght Pack—'the finest in Ireland or the wo-r-r-r-ld.' Not far distant on higher ground were the walls of an ancient mansion, dignified by the title of Castle Kelly, which had been in the family for ages. If ever the Kellys—who dropped their 'O' in 1690—had been as high up the hill as the ruins were, they were going down very rapidly—indeed, they were very nearly at the bottom of it at the time of my birth."

Russell managed to take a cheerful view of his family's diminished fortunes. An aunt, he once recalled, "left me a sum of money in her will, but it could never be found anywhere else." When his father's business failed, the boy was sent to live with his maternal grandfather, the boisterous fox hunter, Captain Jack.

"All my early memories," Russell wrote, "were related to hounds, horses and hunting; there were hounds all over the place, horses in the fields and men on horseback galloping, blowing of horns, cracking of whips, tallyho-ing yoicksing and general uproar."

Unfortunately, Captain Jack had more talent for roaring out hunting songs than he had for managing his finances. The horses and hounds were soon taken away and the estate sold off to pay his debts. His bewildered grandson left Lily Vale for Dublin, where he moved into his grandfather Russell's spacious brick house on Upper Baggot Street.

There, at the age of sixteen, William Russell undertook his first assignment as a newspaper reporter. Spying a curious-looking lark in a neighboring churchyard, he shot the bird, traced its corpse on a sheet of paper, wrote a lengthy description of its appearance, and delivered the opus to the editor of the Dublin *Penny Journal.*

Much to Russell's surprise, the story was published the following week under the impressive headline "ALAUDA CRISTATA FOUND IN IRELAND." The paper identified the bird as a rare specimen of crested lark.

After reading and rereading the story a dozen times at the stationer's shop, Russell took a copy of the *Journal* home and casually mentioned to his grandparents that a strange bird had been discovered in the area. They showed not the slightest interest in the news.

"I daresay it was Jenny Osborne's parrot," one of his aunts remarked. "It escaped last week."

Russell's comfortable life in Dublin ended abruptly when his grandfather died in 1836. The Russells, he discovered then, were as close to the bottom of the hill as the Kellys had been.

Somehow his grandmother and aunts scraped together enough money to pay the boy's tuition at Trinity College, but soon after his twentieth birthday, and long before he was ready to take his degree, they began to have second thoughts about the expense. From time to time, William would be reminded that he ought to be "up and stirring"—although he could not resist pointing out that no one had any suggestion as to what he should be up to or what he should stir.

The problem was solved when one of his cousins arrived from England and offered Russell a job reporting on the forthcoming Irish elections for the London *Times*. The job paid one guinea—about five dollars—a day, and Russell could start the following week.

It was a hectic assignment. The Irish Catholics detested their English Protestant landlords and the political gatherings frequently erupted into riots and brawls. Russell attended one committee meeting at which brick and paving stones came crashing through the windows and bounced off the conference table inside. On another occasion, he was seen chatting with the Tory candidate outside a hotel in Athlone and was promptly seized by a horde of angry Irish housewives who scratched, pinched, and slapped him, then tried to hurl him into the River Shannon.

Russell seemed to thrive on the excitement. He wrote such lively descriptions of the campaign that, when the elections were over, he was summoned to London and offered a regular job with the *Times*. The post was only a temporary one as far as the Dubliner was concerned. He had started studying law in his spare time, and his marriage to nineteen-year-old Mary Burrowes in 1846 made him even more determined to abandon Printing House Square for more lucrative work in the London courts.

Then, in October, 1853, Czar Nicholas I of Russia ordered his armies to march on the Turkish Empire. The attack was supposedly precipitated by a dispute between Turkish police and Russian Orthodox monks at the Christian shrines in the Holy Land, but in reality the czar had long been looking for an excuse to conquer his weaker neighbor to the south.

Although British sympathies lay with the Turks, William Howard Russell had no inkling that England was actually going to intervene in the struggle until he was called into John Delane's office that February evening. He saw at once that his editor was offering him a unique opportunity. The would-be attorney dropped his law books and the adventurous reporter began sharpening his pencils. Kissing his wife and baby daughter good-bye, William Howard Russell prepared to sail for the East.

The *Times* had received assurances from the War Department that its correspondent would be welcome to join the British Expeditionary Army. Somehow, news of the department's approval never reached the army's field commanders.

At a camp in Turkey one general discovered Russell's tent pitched beside a contingent of Coldstream Guards and promptly ordered his aides to pull it down. On another occasion, the reporter made an appointment with British commander in chief in the East, Lord Raglan, but when he arrived for the interview he was told that his lordship was "very much engaged."

"Lord Raglan has determined not to recognize the press in any way," Russell wrote back to John T. Delane, "or to give them rations or assistance and worse than all, it is too probable that he will forbid our accompanying the troops."

Still, Russell managed to find a bright spot in the picture. "Perhaps, after all," he remarked later, "the state of correspondents who were treated in this way was the more gracious; they were freer agents than they have become since under military censorship with tickets and badges."

Despite Lord Raglan's lack of cooperation, the *Times* correspondent managed to find himself a horse, "a fiddle-headed, ewe-necked beast with great bone and not much else." Notebook and pencil in hand, he rode all through the British camp and, following his paper's motto, "The Truth in All Things," described in detail the conditions he saw.

Strangely, no provisions had been made for the arrival of a full-scale army in Turkey. Officers as well as privates were without beds, and none of the soldiers had more than a single regulation blanket to protect him against the freezing temperatures at night. Food supplies were practically non-existent. Eggs and milk were luxuries and the little meat that was available to the British had the texture, said Russell, of "coarse mahogany."

Even more appalling was the problem of disease. Small-pox, cholera, and dysentery were rampant. "The worst thing I have to report is the continued want of comforts for the sick," Russell said. There was no equipment for setting up a base hospital, and dying men remained in camp without so much as a drop of medicine to relieve their suffering.

The first major battle of the Crimean War took place at the Alma River on September 20. The day before the engagement, Russell was approached by an army officer who informed him that General Pennefather wanted to know who he was and what he was doing in the camp. When Russell appeared in the general's headquarters and explained that he was a newspaper reporter, Pennefather exploded with rage.

"I had as soon see the devil!" he thundered angrily. "What

do you know about this kind of work, and what will you do when we get into action?"

"It is quite true that I have very little acquaintance with the business," the civilian replied calmly, "but I suspect that there are a great many here with no greater knowledge than myself."

"Begad, you're right," the general exclaimed delightedly. "You're an Irishman, I'll be bound, and what's your name, sir?"

Russell introduced himself and the two men chatted cordially for a few minutes. When they were finished, General Pennefather agreed to allow Russell to remain with the army, but he warned him that it would be a dangerous mission. "Keep away from the front," he advised sternly, "if you don't want to have your nose cut short."

Years later, William Howard Russell reminded General Pennefather of their first encounter. "Do you know," Pennefather chuckled, "I often thought afterwards what a comfort it would have been to the Government if I had put you in charge of the provost and sent you on board ship. Mind, I'm glad I didn't do it anyway."

When the Cossacks charged the next day, the reporter was on hand for the battle. Shells burst all around him and shots bounced off the ground at his feet. Astride his broken-down horse, scribbling as fast as he could, Rusell's only concern was finding the best spot from which to view the fighting. Later, he wrote his dispatches on pages torn from an old notebook, using a plank laid across two casks for a desk.

Victorious at the Alma, the British forces advanced to the Black Sea port of Balaklava. The little town with its tile-roofed villas and colorful gardens was a popular Turkish summer resort, but when twenty-five thousand British soldiers suddenly descended on it the town's charm vanished overnight.

"Words cannot describe its filth, its horrors, its hospitals, its burials . . ." William Howard Russell wrote of Balaklava. "The town is in a filthy, revolting state. Lord Raglan has ordered it to be cleansed, but there is no one to obey the order and no one attends to it."

Again, there were no hospitals, no medicines, no doctors. Men died without the least effort having been made to save them. "The sick appear to be tended by the sick," said Russell, "and the dying by the dying." He pleaded for doctors to aid the stricken troops, but even more desperate, he said, was the need for nurses. "Are there no devoted women among us," the *Times* man asked, "able and willing to go forth and minister to the sick and suffering soldiers?"

Back in London, a spinster named Florence Nightingale read Russell's words and promptly organized a corps of thirty-eight nurses to tend the men in the Crimea. Her efforts marked the beginning of nursing as a recognized profession. Some historians claim that this was the only positive result of an otherwise pointless war.

The allied army at Balaklava was woefully short of troops and supplies. Out of 35,600 men, only 16,500 were fit for duty. Nevertheless, the Redcoats massed for battle, and on the morning of October 25 the Russians attacked. The scene of the fighting was a wide plain just south of Sevastopol. It was surrounded by hills, many of them so infested with Russian artillery that the Englishmen had dubbed it the Valley of Death.

Russell watched the battle from the British-held heights on the opposite side of the plain. The Russian cavalry advanced down the hill. Gathering speed at every stride, they charged forward against the British line, "that thin red streak topped with a line of steel." As the British Heavy Brigade of Cavalry under General Lucan met the Russians full force, a new line of enemy troops was forming in the hills beyond.

"And now occurred that melancholy catastrophe which fills us all with sorrow," Russell wrote. Lord Cardigan, the general in command of the Light Brigade of Cavalry, on orders from General Lucan, gave the order for his men to advance. The brigade numbered 607 men. They would have to ride a mile and a half in full range of the enemy's fire. On the far side of the already bloody plain Russell could see the second wave of Russians. Their first line alone was double the length of the British line and at least three times as deep. Lord Cardigan's cavalry saw the enemy, too, but not one of them hesitated.

"They swept proudly past," Russell said, "glittering in the morning sun in all the pride and splendor of the war. We could scarcely believe the evidence of our senses! Surely that handful of men are not going to charge an enemy in position? Alas! It was but too true—their desperate valor knew no bounds and far indeed was it removed from its so-called better part, discretion. They advanced in two lines, quickening their pace as they closed toward the enemy. A more fearful spectacle was never witnessed than by those who, without power to aid, beheld their heroic countrymen rushing to the arms of death. At the distance of 1,200 yards the whole line of the enemy belched forth, from thirty iron mouths, a flood of smoke and flame, through which hissed the deadly balls. Their flight was marked by instant gaps in our ranks, by dead men and horses, by steeds flying wounded or riderless across the plain."

When the charge ended at 11:35 Russell reported, "not a British soldier, except the dead and dying, was left in front of those bloody Muscovite guns . . . Our loss, as far as it could be ascertained in killed, wounded and missing at two o'clock today, was as follows: 607 went into action, 198 returned from action: loss, 409."

William Howard Russell's description of the daring but futile cavalry charge was mailed off to England. It appeared in the *Times* two weeks later and sent the entire nation into mourning. His story is credited with inspiring Lord Tennyson's poem *The Charge of the Light Brigade*. Still another English writer, Rudyard Kipling, readily admitted that he borrowed Russell's words, "that thin red streak topped with a line of steel," and changed them to his more famous "thin red line of heroes" in the poem *Tommy*.

Meanwhile, Russell's reporting of the scandalous conditions in the Crimea had aroused the British people to a bitter protest against the conduct of the war. Shiploads of medical and military supplies finally began steaming through the Mediterranean to Turkey. The *Times* reporter, said one military authority, had awakened "the conscience of the British nation to the sufferings of its troops."

In the fall of 1855, the war ended with the capture of the Russian forces at Sevastopol and William Howard Russell returned home in a blaze of glory. The new prime minister, Lord Palmerston, received him at breakfast, and in Dublin, Trinity College awarded him an honorary LL.D.—the degree of doctor of laws.

Now that Russell had demonstrated his talents as a war correspondent, John T. Delane took advantage of every opportunity to use them. In 1857, Dr. Russell, as he was now called, went to India to cover the Sepoy Rebellion. He wrote a number of dispatches in which he forthrightly criticized British officials for their cruel treatment of the mutinous native troops.

Four years later, the world-famous correspondent was off to the United States. He was welcomed by no less a person than Abraham Lincoln. "The London *Times*," said the president, "is one of the greatest powers in the world—in fact, I don't know anything which has much more power—except the Mississippi. I am glad to know you as its Minister."

Lincoln might have been even more cordial if the mighty *Times* had supported his stand against secession. However, the paper's sympathies were entirely with the South, although Russell himself professed to be neutral.

Russell was in Charleston, South Carolina, on that fateful April day when the Confederates fired on Fort Sumter. He was also at Bull Run, the first major battle of the Civil War. There he watched unseasoned federal troops fleeing in the face of a powerful rebel attack. The Blues had stood up to the Grays in the early stages of the fighting, and most of the American correspondents raced back to Washington with news of a Union victory. Russell, more experienced as a war reporter, waited until later in the day. By then he had an almost unbelievable scene to describe:

"Infantry soldiers on mules and draught horses, with the harness clinging to their heels, as much frightened as their riders; Negro servants on their masters' chargers; ambulances crowded with unwounded soldiers; wagons swarming with men who threw out the contents on the road to make more room, grinding through a screaming, shouting mass of men on foot, who were literally yelling with rage at every halt . . ."

Russell's faithful reporting of the rout prompted a storm of angry denunciations from the North. One newspaper blasted him as "the snob correspondent of the London *Times*." Another called him a "bilious LL.D."

The reporter was soon declaring that he was "the best

abused man in America." To add to his woes, his popularity in England also plummeted after he had the audacity to suggest to his pro-southern readers that defeat of the Confederacy was inevitable. Hounded on both sides of the Atlantic for his attempts to tell "'the truth in all things,'" Russell finally handed in his resignation and sailed for home.

In recognition of his past services, the *Times* awarded Russell a generous pension, and he settled down to become the editor of his own paper, the *Army and Navy Gazette*. His career as a war correspondent was not completely over, however. In 1870, the *Times* asked him to return to work to report on the Franco-Prussian War, and in 1879 he went to South Africa to cover the Zulu War for the *Daily Telegraph*.

In both instances, Russell's dispatches were as astute and vividly worded as ever, but editors grumbled because he insisted on putting style ahead of speed. While other correspondents were dashing off hasty releases and scrambling to the telegraph office, Russell would still be in his quarters, leisurely writing out a long story that would have to be sent by mail.

As far as Russell was concerned, the new methods of transmitting news took most of the fun out of reporting. "The electric telegraph," he grumbled, "quite annihilates one's speculative and inductive faculties. What's the use of trying to find out where an expedition is going to, when, long before the result of one's investigation can reach England, not only the destination but the results of that expedition will be known from John o'Groat's to Land's End?"

Knighted in 1895, Dr. Russell became Sir William Russell. A few years later he received the prestigious emblem of Commander of the Royal Victorian Order. His warm friend and admirer, King Edward VII, conferred the honor. "You must not trouble to kneel, Billy," the king admonished the now portly, white-maned journalist. "Stoop!"

In 1907, shortly before his eighty-seventh birthday, Russell died and was buried in the crypt of London's St. Paul's Cathedral. The grave is marked by a striking bronze statue of the reporter in his prime, pencil poised above his notebook, campaign cloak flung over his shoulders. "SIR WILLIAM HOWARD RUSSELL, LL.D.," says the marble legend at the base of the statue, "THE FIRST AND GREATEST OF WAR CORRESPONDENTS."

2

George Washburn Smalley

William Howard Russell was the first newspaperman to
follow an army into battle, but it was an American journalist,
George Washburn Smalley, who added a new and important dimension to the war correspondent's craft—the dimension of speed. Writing in the early days of the telegraph and
the transatlantic cable, Smalley was the first to use both
inventions for transmitting news stories.

On the basis of his appearance and personality alone,
George Smalley was the perfect war correspondent. A tall
man with powerful shoulders and a determined jaw, he had
a quick mind, iron nerves, and a firm commitment to whatever task he set out to accomplish. But aside from these
qualities, there was little in Smalley's background to qualify
him as a journalist.

He was born in the small town of Franklin, Massachusetts,
in 1833, but his family moved to Worcester a few years later
when his father became pastor of the Second Congregational
Church there. Worcester at that time was a sedate New
England village with quiet, elm-shaded streets and plain
but sturdy houses, most of them dating back to colonial days.

Like most of the other boys in Worcester, George Smalley learned to swim and fish, to fly kites and climb trees. With less enthusiasm, he also went off to the town academy to study Latin and Greek and prepare for the entrance examinations at Yale.

The capacity for hard work that later made Smalley so successful as a newspaperman was scarcely visible during his college days. His grades were mediocre, and his main claim to distinction was that he was a member of the Yale crew that, in 1852, rowed in the first Yale-Harvard race on Lake Winnipesaukee, New Hampshire. Unfortunately, Harvard won.

The Reverend Mr. Smalley and his wife Louisa Jane wanted their son to become a lawyer. George could think of no reason not to do as they wished. After graduating from Yale he began reading law in the office of George Frisbie Hoar, a distinguished attorney who later became a member of the United States Senate. The work was interesting enough to inspire George Smalley to take a degree at Harvard Law School. He was admitted to the bar in 1856, but his career as a lawyer was to be a brief one.

Smalley joined a law firm in Boston where he met and became friends with Wendell Phillips, the noted reformer. An outspoken foe of slavery, Phillips enlisted the young lawyer in his crusade for abolition. When the Civil War broke out in 1861, he also arranged for Smalley to cover the fighting as a special correspondent for the *New York Tribune*.

The journalists who covered the Civil War were popularly known at the Bohemian Brigade. Most of them were footloose adventurers with a taste for whiskey and a nose for news. Smalley, with his degrees from Harvard and Yale and his proper Boston manners, stood out from the crowd.

When it came to reporting, however, he was easily their equal.

Smalley rode into the Shenandoah Valley with General John Frémont and was later in Virginia with General John Pope. On one occasion, General Pope decided to make his own reconnaissance of the enemy's position. Smalley and a small force of soldiers went with him. Without realizing it, the general passed some distance beyond his own lines and, when he and his men tried to return to camp, they were immediately attacked by the Union forces who thought Pope and his scouting party were the enemy.

Smalley found himself charging through a hail of bullets on the back of a horse that was even more frightened than he was. Miraculously, no one in the general's party was hit, but, as Smalley said later, "A good many remarks were made which hit General Pope."

The special correspondent's dispatches to the *Tribune* turned out to be of no more than routine interest. Then one day he heard a rumor that General George McClellan might soon be fighting an important engagement not far from Washington. Expecting to be gone a day or two, Smalley took only his raincoat and a toothbrush. It was six weeks before he returned to the capital. In the interval he performed what many authorities consider the greatest journalistic feat of the Civil War.

In those days, most officers saw little need for war correspondents. They were, in fact, forbidden to be with an army in the field. Smalley went along with McClellan's troops not as a reporter but as a volunteer aide-de-camp to General John Sedgwick. Sedgwick, well aware of Smalley's real mission, never called for his services.

In September, 1862, General Robert E. Lee made his first attempt to invade the North. George McClellan and an army of seventy thousand Union troops were sent by President Abraham Lincoln to turn him back. The first encounter was at South Mountain, not far from Frederick, Maryland, where McClellan's forces routed Lee's rear guard. Smalley watched the battle on horseback only a few feet away from where the commanding general stood. McClellan never once suspected that he was sharing his vantage point with a member of the press. Once Smalley even offered the general his field glasses, but McClellan declined, saying he could see very well already.

After the defeat at South Mountain, Lee rallied his forces and withdrew to a position in the Maryland countryside just beyond Antietam Creek. It was obvious that there was going to be a major battle.

Smalley was anxious to find out where he stood the best chance of seeing some action. Hearing that General "Fighting Joe" Hooker was planning a flank attack on the enemy's left, Smalley rode over and attached himself to Hooker's staff command. "Nobody took the trouble to ask who I was or why I was there," he said later. "For aught they knew I might have been a rebel spy."

The army moved into position at nightfall and the men flopped on the ground for an uneasy sleep. "At four o'clock next morning," said Smalley, "with the earliest light of a coming dawn and as soon as a man could see the sights on his rifle, the battle began."

"Fighting Joe" Hooker was the first man in the saddle, but George Washburn Smalley was not far behind him. The general spent almost the entire morning on the firing line. Once, at the height of the battle, he was searching for an officer to carry a message to one of his regiments. Catching sight of Smalley, he promptly pressed him into service. For the next few hours, the correspondent was kept busy riding back and forth delivering orders from Hooker to his officers.

When he rode up to the colonel of one regiment with the general's order to march to the front, the man insisted that he could not comply because the order was delivered by a civilian rather than a staff officer.

"Very good," replied Smalley, "I will report to General Hooker that you decline to obey."

"Oh, for God's sake, don't do that!" cried the colonel. "The rebels are too many for us, but I had rather face them than Hooker."

Smalley stayed with Hooker from the beginning of the battle at dawn until nine o'clock when the general, wounded in the foot by a rebel sharpshooter, was taken to a small, red brick schoolhouse at the rear of the Union lines. The correspondent returned to the battlefield and remained there until late that evening, when Lee's advance was finally stopped. On that day more men were killed and wounded than on any other day of the Civil War. The South suffered approximately 10,000 casualties and the North about 12,000.

When the battle ended, there were bullet holes in George Smalley's clothes, and his horse had been shot out from under him. But he had seen the invasion of the North repulsed. It was the first victory for the Union since the war began.

The army's work was done, but George Smalley's was just beginning. Borrowing a horse from another newspaperman, he rode off to Frederick, Maryland, reaching there at three in the morning. An important battle had been fought less than thirty miles away, but to Smalley's consternation no one had the slightest interest in relaying the news to the rest of the country. The telegraph office was shut tight and no one even knew where the operator lived.

Smalley waited impatiently until seven the following

morning, when the telegraph clerk finally arrived and unlocked the door. When the correspondent told him what he wanted, the man agreed to get the message through. Smalley sat down on a log by the front door and began writing the story of the battle of Antietam Creek.

The clerk started clicking out the words on his telegraph but, instead of going directly to New York as Smalley had believed it would, the story was intercepted in Washington, D.C. It was the first coherent account of the battle to reach either the War Department or President Lincoln. Eventually the news got to New York, where it appeared on the front page of the *Tribune,* the only paper in the country with the story.

The battle of Antietam Creek had ended late in the day on Friday, September 17. Smalley's first brief account appeared on Saturday, but he also hoped to write a more detailed version that would be on the newsstands by Sunday morning. It was an unheard-of deadline. At that time news was considered new if it was published within a week or two of the actual event.

Smalley knew that his one hope of making the Sunday headlines was to write his story and carry it to New York in person. It took hours for him to secure a seat on the train out of Frederick. Then he arrived in Baltimore with only a few minutes in which to dash across the platform and hop aboard the express to New York.

That night, in a rattling railroad coach, Smalley wrote his historic story. ". . . by the light of the one dim oil lamp, above my head, standing, I began a narrative of the battle of Antietam," he said later. "I wrote with pencil. It must have been about nine o'clock when I began. I ended as the train rolled into Jersey City by daylight."

Smalley had managed to telegraph the editor of the *Tri-*

bune that he and his story were on the way. The proof-readers and compositors were waiting to set it up in type. They started work at 6:00 A.M., and by breakfast time on that same Sunday morning, September 19, the *Tribune* had issued an extra with six columns on what George Smalley called "the greatest fight since Waterloo." His job done, the journalist turned around and headed back to the battlefields that night.

Smalley's rapid reporting on the battle of Antietam was the most spectacular news story of the day, but his career as a Civil War correspondent was cut short when he was stricken with "camp fever," an infection that plagued many of the troops on both sides of the fight. He returned to New York and after his recovery was assigned to the *Tribune* office to write about the war from a much safer distance.

On Christmas Day, 1862, Smalley married a young widow named Phoebe Garnaut, who was the adopted daughter of his good friend Wendell Phillips. The couple had five children—two boys and three girls.

Four years after his marriage the young husband again became a war correspondent. In June of 1866 a letter arrived at the *Tribune* office with the news that Austria and Prussia were at war. The managing editor handed the message to Smalley. "I want you to take the first steamer to Europe," he said.

The first steamer left two days later and George Washburn Smalley was on it. The Austro-Prussian War, however, lasted only seven weeks. By the time the first news of the clash reached the United States, the war was half over, and by the time the *Tribune* correspondent's boat reached the coast of Ireland, the two countries were on the verge of negotiating a peace treaty.

Still hoping for a story, Smalley went on to Berlin, where

he discovered that there had been a crisis at the conference table. From all accounts, the Prussian army would once again be on the march. The possible resumption of the war was a good news story, and George Smalley decided to try and get it back to his paper in record time.

It was then August 1. On July 28, Queen Victoria had used the recently completed transatlantic cable to send a message to President Andrew Johnson. The president had cabled back a reply that arrived in London the next day. Leaving Berlin, Smalley headed straight for the English cable office with his story. His report of the temporary breakdown in the Austro-Prussian peace talks became the first news dispatch to be sent by cable. It consisted of a hundred words and cost five hundred dollars—a rate of five dollars per word. "We wasted no words at that price," Smalley said bluntly.

Despite the ridiculously high cost of sending messages, the transatlantic cable was obviously going to revolutionize the business of reporting foreign news. Smalley had still another plan to bring Europe and the United States in closer touch. He asked the editor of the *Tribune* to let him set up an office in London where he could receive dispatches from newspapermen in all the major cities of Europe and transmit them directly to New York.

The editor was skeptical, but he agreed to let Smalley try it. In the spring of 1867, Smalley was given the title of foreign commissioner and authorized to organize the first overseas news bureau ever set up by an American newspaper. The innovation caused no great stir in newspaper circles until the summer of 1870, when France and Prussia went to war. Newspaper readers in the United States suddenly wanted instant reports from the battlefield.

The editor of the *Tribune*, who still did not completely understand his foreign commissioner's plans for a central news office, ordered Smalley to Berlin to cover the war at close range. Smalley ignored the order, and instead sent other journalists into the field while he remained in London to forward their dispatches to New York.

Transatlantic rates were still exorbitant, but by now George Smalley was so convinced of the cable's efficiency that he was determined to ignore the price. In the six months' long Franco-Prussian War, he managed to run up a bill of over $125,000 for news dispatches.

English journalists scoffed at Smalley's methods. They refused to believe that a story of any length could be transmitted by wire. To them the telegraph was good only for communicating the results of a battle. The full story was to be written by hand and sent on by mail. Smalley disagreed. The whole point of reporting, as he saw it, was to have several good columns of news and to get it to the reader as quickly as possible. He proved his point to the rest of the newspaper world after the battle of Sedan (a French town near the Belgian border).

The battle was fought on Thursday, September 1, 1870. It ended in a French rout and the surrender of Sedan. News of the battle reached London on Saturday, but there were no details—the only word was that it had occurred and Prussia had won. But Smalley had no use for such general facts. He wanted a complete story, and by five o'clock that afternoon he was on his way to getting it.

Smalley had sent the two best reporters he could find into action. One was an Englishman, Holt White, the other a Frenchman named Mejanel. White rode with the Prussians, Mejanel with his own countrymen. The foreign commissioner had ordered both reporters to go directly to the front. If they witnessed a minor skirmish, they were to telegraph the news to London without delay. If there was a major engagement, he knew they would have a hard time finding an open line. In that case, they were to start for London themselves, writing their accounts along the way.

Both White and Mejanel were at the final battle of Sedan. It was a spectacular defeat for France. Three thousand of their troops were killed and twenty-one thousand were taken prisoner, including the emperor, Napoleon III.

At five o'clock on Saturday afternoon, two days after the battle, Holt White staggered into Smalley's office, dirty and bedraggled—"a mere wreck of a correspondent," as Smalley described him. White had walked across the still smoldering battlefield, talked his way past both the Prussian and the French lines, and had ridden halfway across Belgium on horseback. He had hoped to find a telegraph station when he reached Brussels, but the operators there knew nothing of the defeat at Sedan and, thinking White was a madman, refused to send his story to London.

Luckily, White found a train that took him as far as Calais, France. From there he caught the boat to Dover and then chartered a special train to take him to London. In the midst of his frantic traveling, he had not had time to write one word of his story. Moreover, he had had neither food nor sleep for hours. When he finally staggered into the *Tribune* office, he swore he could not write a single line.

George Smalley ignored the statement. "A continent was waiting for the news locked up in that man's brain," he said later, "and somehow or other the lock must be forced, the news told."

Smalley could be totally ruthless when a news story was at stake.

"You shall have something to eat," he told the exhausted

correspondent, "but sleep you shall not till you have done your dispatch. That must be in New York tomorrow morning."

With that the foreign commissioner took his reporter by the arm and propelled him out of the office to a small restaurant not far away. They were back at Smalley's desk in less than an hour.

Even Holt White was somewhat confused about his boss's methods of cabling news. He assumed, in the British tradition, that his story would have to be condensed as much as possible.

Smalley shook his head. "Not at all," he said.

"But—it's going by cable," White stammered.

"Yes."

"And it will be several columns long?"

"The longer the better," Smalley replied blandly.

White was still baffled. "Please put the cable out of your mind," Smalley finally told him, "and write exactly as if you were writing for a London paper with the printer's devil waiting."

There were no further problems. Holt White wrote a clear and vivid account of everything he had seen at Sedan. He finished at midnight, and by two in the morning the last page had been put on the wire to New York. It was published in the *Tribune* in time for the first edition on Sunday morning. No other paper in the United States had such a complete account of the battle and, in London, none appeared until the following Tuesday morning.

Meanwhile, Smalley's other correspondent, Mejanel, arrived in England on Monday afternoon. He had been taken prisoner by the French, but had escaped and made his way back to London. Although he was almost as exhausted as Holt White had been, he wrote a lively account of his view of the battle from inside the French lines. On Tuesday, while Londoners were just reading the first details of Sedan, the *New York Tribune* had already printed its second exclusive story on the battle.

England was considered the world's leader in journalism, and every newspaper editor in the country was embarrassed by Smalley's scoops. He had paid a small fortune in cable fees to report the Franco-Prussian War (which led to the creation of the German Empire), but the *Tribune* had more than earned it back in sales and prestige.

Smalley remained head of the *Tribune's* Europe office until 1895. He then took a position as American correspondent for the London *Times,* doing most of his reporting from New York City and Washington, D.C. Later he retired to London, where he lived until his death in 1916 at the age of eighty-three.

George Washburn Smalley has earned a high place in newspaper history for his insistence on placing speed beside accuracy in the correspondent's credo. His use of the telegraph in the Civil War and the transatlantic cable in the Franco-Prussian War are landmarks in the transmission of news. But Smalley took little of the credit for himself and considered it instead a triumph for his country and his paper.

"I think we are entitled to remember with satisfaction," he said, "that in telegraphic news enterprise, even in Europe, it was an American journal which led the way and that the *Tribune* was that journal."

3

Henry Wing

Friday, May 6, 1864, was a pleasant day in Washington, D.C., but few people could enjoy the balmy spring weather. Three days before, President Abraham Lincoln had ordered General Ulysses S. Grant and an army of 150,000 men to begin a march toward the Confederate capital at Richmond, Virginia. It was a decisive move. If the Army of the Potomac could break through General Robert E. Lee's defenses, they would be on their way to capturing the capital and ending the Civil War.

Grant and his troops had left their headquarters at Culpeper, Virginia, very early on Tuesday morning. They had crossed the Rapidan River that afternoon and Grant had wired his commander in chief: "Forty-eight hours now will demonstrate whether the enemy intends giving battle this side of Richmond."

The telegram was the last word anyone had heard from Ulysses Grant. His army seemed to have vanished from the face of the earth. Had the enemy given battle? Had Grant won? Or had his army been defeated? Were rebel troops even now storming north to capture Washington?

It was hardly surprising that Friday was an anxious day for the residents of the nation's capital. The city was rife with rumors. According to one report, several northern regiments had been completely wiped out. In some places, the whispered word was that Lee's men would be marching up Pennsylvania Avenue in less than twenty-four hours.

Abraham Lincoln had spent the better part of those tense three days in the telegraph office of the War Department. He had staked his political future and the future of the Union on Grant's ability to continue his advance toward Richmond. He had to know whether or not Grant was going to make it.

Early Saturday morning, Abraham Lincoln finally received his first news of General Grant and the Army of the Potomac. It did not arrive in the War Department telegraph office. It came instead from the lips of a grimy and disheveled young war correspondent named Henry Wing.

Wing had made a daring escape through Confederate lines and arrived in Washington with a story that not only put an anxious country at ease, but also made headlines for the *New York Tribune* and turned the youthful journalist into a close friend of the President of the United States.

Lincoln's favorite reporter was born in 1840 in the small town of Goshen in northwestern Connecticut. In that remote country village, just as in every other section of the country, the burning issue of the day was slavery. Henry Wing had grown up exposed to two different points of view on the subject. His father, a minister, was a staunch abolitionist with no tolerance for anyone who questioned his views. His mother, however, had been a teacher on a southern plantation before her marriage. The lot of the slaves, she told her son, was not nearly as bad as her husband insisted.

Henry, who did not get along with his father, was inclined to accept his mother's opinion. But he began to change his mind when he grew older and became a teacher at a boarding school in Vermont. Henry had frequently maintained that it was foolish for a black man to run away, and that if he knew of an escaping slave he would consider it his duty to send him back to his master.

One day, a Negro boy named Jake who worked at the school came to the young teacher and asked him if he really meant what he said. The schoolmaster assured him that he did, but when Jake confessed that he was a runaway and his master was after him, Henry Wing knew that he could never be so heartless. "Jake," he promised, "they shall not get you." Wing not only found someone to take the boy across the border to Canada; he also gave him most of his savings to pay his way.

Henry Wing was just twenty-one years old when the South attacked Fort Sumter in the spring of 1861. He had strong feelings about preserving the Union and he was quick to enlist in the army. His regiment was the Twenty-Seventh Connecticut Volunteers, and Henry was proud to be chosen as a member of the color guard.

The Twenty-Seventh's first major battle was at Fredericksburg in the winter of 1862. It was a bloody defeat for the Union. Over thirteen thousand men were killed or wounded—among the latter Henry Wing. He was cut down by a volley of shots early in the fighting and woke up some hours later to find himself lying on top of a piano in a makeshift emergency hospital. Several doctors were standing over him, and Henry looked down to see a mark around his leg and another around his arm. He knew at once that they were about to be amputated.

Infuriated, Henry began to denounce the doctors so loudly that they lifted him off the piano and threw him out on the grass. "You couldn't blame them," he said later. "There were twelve doctors for fifteen hundred wounded men and they couldn't have patients fighting them. They didn't think I would live anyway."

Eventually someone found time to rescue the wounded man and move him from the emergency ward to a regular hospital. No one made any further attempt to treat his shattered arm and leg. Instead, one of the Sisters of Charity who ran the hospital asked if she could get him a priest or a minister. "Does that mean you think I'm going to die?" asked Wing suspiciously.

The nun nodded. "You cannot live overnight," she told him.

Henry Wing refused to believe her. "Before I left home," he said to the nun, "my mother read from the Ninety-First Psalm: *A thousand shall fall at thy side, and ten thousand at thy right hand; but it shall not come nigh thee.* 'You are coming back, Henry,' she said. You don't suppose that I am going to die after that, do you?"

The nun was so impressed by the soldier's faith that she assigned a special nun to take care of him. His wounds were carefully bathed and dressed and, although two of his fingers had to be amputated, his arm and leg were saved. It took him almost three months to recover, but eventually he was discharged from the hospital. He limped slightly as a result of his leg wound, but otherwise he was very much alive and able to resume a normal life.

Despite Wing's painful experience as a soldier, he was more devoted than ever to the Union cause. Not all of his neighbors in Connecticut shared his commitment to the

Civil War. When Wing returned home, he began making speeches and writing editorials urging them to support President Lincoln and the fight against secession.

Several of his columns in the local paper came to the attention of Horace Greeley, the editor of the *New York Tribune,* who soon invited him to join his staff. Wing was happy to accept the post, and happier still when he managed to get assigned to the newspaper's Washington office. He would be closer to the battlefields there and perhaps he could eventually rejoin the army as a war correspondent.

Soon after Wing's arrival in Washington, however, the entire corps of *Tribune* reporters retreated from the field. They were being pursued not by rebels, but by the secretary of war, Edwin Stanton. The secretary had been carrying on a personal battle against war correspondents ever since the firing on Fort Sumter. In some cases, his hostility was justified. The army's movements were supposed to be kept secret, but the newsmen, anxious for a good story, insisted on reporting them to the entire country. Sometimes, too, the reporters would curry favor among the officers. In exchange for information, they would give a particular general more than his just share of headlines.

Secretary Stanton had already issued an order forbidding correspondents to accompany the army into battle. It was generally disregarded. In complete exasperation, the secretary finally announced that civilians were not to be allowed anywhere near the front. This time he meant it and the correspondents, to a man, obeyed.

Sam Wilkeson, the chief of the *Tribune*'s Washington bureau, alternately threatened and pleaded with his reporters to violate the War Department edict, but not one of them dared risk Stanton's wrath. The penalty for disobedience would be a long and uncomfortable term in an army prison.

Henry Wing, still hungering to become a war correspondent, decided to take a chance. He sneaked out of Washington, made his way past the Union pickets, and joined the Army of the Potomac in its winter quarters at Culpeper. When he sent Sam Wilkeson a wire with the news of his whereabouts, Wilkeson rewarded him with an on-the-spot promotion to field correspondent.

A few weeks later, several more newsmen, inspired by Wing's feat, attached themselves to General Grant's forces. The reporters were still with them when President Lincoln ordered Grant to advance on Richmond. During those three nerve-racking days, while the whole nation waited for news from Virginia, Henry Wing and his fellow reporters were witnessing a momentous battle.

After crossing the Rapidan River and passing through open country near Chancellorsville, the Union soldiers had to make their way through a dense tangle of bushes and forest that was known as the Wilderness. Suddenly, Lee ordered his men out of their entrenchments for a full-scale attack. The Battle of the Wilderness had begun.

At the end of the second day's fighting, the *Tribune* men assembled in Grant's headquarters. They agreed that one of them should try to take a dispatch back to Washington; the one they selected was Henry Wing. Along with the news of what was happening in the Wilderness, Wing took with him a message from Ulysses Grant with orders to deliver it in person to the president of the United States.

The reporter set out on the seventy-mile trip to Washington at four o'clock that morning. Not sure of the way, he decided to stop at Culpeper and get precise directions from one of his friends there. The man, a Union sympathizer, took one look at Henry Wing and told him he was a fool. Several detachments of Confederate soldiers had come in behind Grant, and the rebels now occupied most of the countryside between there and Washington. Wing would never get by them, "especially in those clothes," the man growled.

The newspaperman was wearing the official uniform of a *Tribune* correspondent—corduroy knickers, a buckskin jacket, and handsome leather boots. His only hope of passing through the Confederate lines was to abandon his fine outfit and go disguised as a field hand. Henry's friend gave him an old shirt, a pair of rough trousers, heavy shoes, and a faded cap. He advised him to pose as a southern field hand hurrying to tell his rebel friends in Washington that Lee had just beaten Grant and was on his way to the capital.

Wing had ridden only a few miles when he met a group of gray-clad soldiers. Faking a southern accent, he told his story. To his relief the men believed him and even offered him a military escort as protection against a chance attack by straggling Yankees. They rode for about a dozen miles until they came to a river crossing called Kelly's Ford. Kelly, who owned the adjacent property, was a dedicated secessionist. Recognizing the Yankee correspondent, he jumped for the newsman's bridle. Just as he did, Wing's horse, named Jess, bounded into the river. Horse and rider escaped upstream amid a hail of shots from their former protectors.

There were more rebel encampments on the other side of the river. But Wing managed to get through them by telling his story and then riding quickly away while the soldiers were still cheering the bogus victory. When he was about thirty miles from Washington, the disguised field hand realized that his best hope of reaching the city was to abandon his horse and try to make the rest of the trip by following the railroad ties. Jess had saved his life with his quick action at Kelly's Ford, and Wing hated to abandon him. He tied him in a secluded thicket, left him a bag of oats, and promised to return as soon as he could.

From there the journalist walked for several hours along the tracks until he came to the Confederate cavalry camp near Manassas Junction. He recited his story once again, but even though the rebels were delighted to hear the good news, they told him there was no need for him to go any farther. They would see that the word got to Washington.

Just to be on the safe side, the Confederate commander ordered the field hand detained in camp. But as soon as it got dark, Henry Wing sneaked away from his captors and followed the railroad tracks for another six miles until he crossed the Union lines and reached the telegraph station at Union Mills.

There Wing discovered that he was the first man to come out of the Wilderness with news of Ulysses Grant. Now he was more determined than ever to get his story back to the *Tribune*. He asked if he could send it by wire, but the operator refused. The War Department would allow nothing but military dispatches to go through. Wing's only hope was to get to Washington himself. He tried to buy a horse, but there was none for sale. Next he offered a thousand dollars for a railroad handcar and a man to run it. But the railroad, he was told, had also been taken over by the army.

Then Wing had a brainstorm. Charles Dana, the first assistant secretary of war, was a former editor of the *New York Tribune*. He persuaded the telegraph clerk to wire Dana and tell him that Wing had just returned from the front and wanted to talk to him.

Unfortunately, Dana was not in his office and the message

went to Secretary of War Stanton. Stanton was outraged when Wing asked for permission to send a telegram to the *Tribune*. Any news from the army, the secretary insisted, should be given directly to him. Suddenly it dawned on Henry Wing that not even the War Department had heard from General Grant. Nevertheless, his first allegiance was to the *Tribune*. He would give Stanton whatever information he wanted, Wing wired back, if he could first send a dispatch to his paper.

The secretary of war was adamant. He not only refused to send the dispatch, but he also threatened to have the man on the other end of the wire shot as a rebel spy.

Fortunately, Abraham Lincoln arrived at the War Department before Stanton's threat could be carried out. His eyes lit up when he heard there was a young man at Union Mills who supposedly had news from the Union army. The president ordered the telegraph operator to contact him at once.

"Is it true that you have come from the army?" Lincoln wanted to know.

"Yes," came Wing's reply.

"What news do you have?"

"I will be happy to tell you," Wing repeated, "if you will first let me send one hundred words to the *Tribune*."

The president's answer came back in minutes. "Write your hundred words and we will send it at once."

True to his promise, Abraham Lincoln let the message go through to New York. Then he offered to send a special train to Union Mills to bring Henry Wing to the White House.

An hour later, Stanton's assistant, Charles Dana, was on his way to escort the twenty-four-year-old correspondent back to Washington. The train arrived soon after one o'clock in the morning and Wing, still in his grimy field hand's clothes, was driven by carriage to the White House.

Abraham Lincoln had summoned all the members of his cabinet to the meeting. The men looked so dismayed at the sight of the mud-splattered figure who was brought before them that for an instant Henry Wing was certain he would be evicted. The secretary of the navy, however—Gideon Wells—was a Connecticut man. Recognizing Wing as one of his neighbors, he stepped forward to shake his hand.

After that, Wing's reception was more cordial. He was invited to sit down and give the president and cabinet officers whatever news he had from General Grant. There was little to tell that had not been in his news dispatch. Grant was fighting Lee in the Wilderness and seemed to be holding his own. Another attack had been planned for the morning that Wing had set off for Washington, but he had no way of knowing whether it had been successful. Disappointed, the cabinet members filed out, but Henry Wing lingered behind.

The president turned to him. "You wanted to speak to me?" he said.

"Yes, Mr. President," Wing replied. "I have a message for you—a message from General Grant. He told me I was to give it to you when you were alone."

The President eyed the young man warily. "Something from Grant to me?" he said.

"Yes," Henry replied. "He told me I was to tell you, Mr. President, that no matter what happens there will be no turning back."

Abraham Lincoln breathed a long sigh of relief. He knew that Ulysses Grant would keep his word. That meant the Union army was on its way to a final victory. On an impulse, the gaunt bearded man from Illinois put his arm around the boy who had brought him the good news and kissed him lightly on the cheek.

Henry Wing's dispatch to the *Tribune* was published later that morning, Saturday, May 7. By then the exhausted newspaperman, still in his muddy clothes, was sprawled on the bed of his room at the National Hotel. He was awakened by the shouts of the newsboys in the street below. "EXTRA EXTRA!" they called. "NEWS FROM THE ARMY. GRANT FOUND!" It was Henry Wing's own story that was causing the excitement.

Henry struggled to his feet and raced the few blocks down the street to his office. He found the place swarming with senators and government officials, all trying to find out if the *Tribune* story was really true. Henry fought his way through the mob and discovered the chief of the Washington bureau, Sam Wilkeson, standing on top of a desk apologizing for the mistake. The story from New York could not possibly be true, he said. The man who was supposed to have sent it was still trapped somewhere in Virginia.

Henry Wing waved his arms wildly. "No, I'm not," he shouted. "Here I am, Mr. Wilkeson.

The astonished crowd immediately swept the reporter off his feet and passed him bodily over their heads to the tabletop where Sam Wilkeson stood. Everyone gave an enthusiastic cheer, and then they passed around a hat that they filled with dollar bills and presented to Henry Wing as a reward for his bravery.

Gradually the crowd in the newspaper office dispersed. Sam Wilkeson turned to his new star reporter and asked him what he was going to do. "If you don't mind," Wing said, "I'll go back to the hotel and get some sleep. I want to be rested because the president has asked me to come and see him again this afternoon."

The young man who appeared at the White House later that day was so clean and well dressed that Abraham Lincoln scarcely recognized him. The president thanked Wing again for delivering the message from Grant and asked if he had any further plans. The reporter replied at once that he was going back to get Jess.

"Jess?" said Lincoln. "Who is Jess?"

Jess, Wing explained, was his horse. He had tied him in a thicket a few miles behind the Confederate lines. "But I can't leave him there," Wing explained. "He's too good a friend for that."

The president nodded. Perhaps, he suggested, there was some way he could help.

Less than twenty-four hours later, Henry Wing was on a train heading south. With him was a battery of soldiers for protection against a possible rebel ambush, and at the rear of the train was a special boxcar and a supply of oats for Jess.

It had been forty-eight hours since Henry Wing left his horse in the woods. In that time anything could have happened. Jess might have been shot or stolen or perhaps had broken his tether and run away. The train squeaked to a halt at the spot where Henry Wing had first started walking along the tracks early Friday morning. He climbed out and plunged into the woods until he found the thicket where he had left his mount. Sure enough, Jess was still there. When he saw his master, he bit the rope that had held him to the tree and let Henry Wing lead him back to the waiting train. They returned to the capital with Jess in his private boxcar, contentedly munching oats along the way.

Once the horse was safe in Washington, the other *Tribune* reporters insisted on buying the animal a new saddle and bridle, which they presented the next day in an unusual ceremony on the White House lawn. That same morning,

Monday, May 9, official word finally came through from Ulysses Grant. The Army of the Potomac had not been defeated. It was still advancing toward Richmond.

Soon after that, Wing rejoined the Union troops and remained with them through the fierce and bloody fighting in that final year of the Civil War. He was popular with the men because of his cheerful good humor. They liked him, too, because he had shared their dangers on the battlefield. His limp and the missing fingers on his left hand attested to that. Nor was he afraid to fight again. In more than one battle, he had grabbed a rifle from a fallen man and fired it in his place.

As a result of Henry Wing's meeting with Abraham Lincoln, he and the president became good friends. Lincoln invited him to visit the White House whenever he was in Washington. From time to time, when there was a lull in the fighting, Wing would return to his room at the National Hotel. When he did, he would also call upon Abraham Lincoln and tell him what was happening at the front. The president had long pages of reports from the War Department, but Henry Wing became his personal correspondent. It was Wing who told him what the soldiers were really thinking and feeling, and how hard and how long they were willing to fight. The information the president received in his private conversations with Henry Wing helped renew his determination to see the war through to the end.

Early in 1865, with a Union victory in sight, Wing began making plans for his own future. He had enjoyed his work on the *Tribune* so much that he decided to edit a newspaper of his own. With the money he had saved from his correspondent's job, he purchased the Litchfield, Connecticut, *Enquirer*. Before he settled down to become an editor, how-

ever, Wing had one wish—to witness the final surrender of
Robert E. Lee.

The reporter returned to the Army of the Potomac for
the final siege at Richmond and saw the first white flag that
fluttered from the Confederate lines. After retreating from
Richmond, Lee was cut off by General Sheridan near a town
called Appomattox Court House and was forced to surrender
unconditionally. When the rumor of the surrender began to
spread through the Union ranks, Wing scored his final scoop.
He arranged with a member of General Grant's staff to signal
him from the porch of the Wilmer McLean house, where
Grant and Lee were meeting to discuss terms.

A large group of soldiers and correspondents had gathered
not far away to wait for the news. Suddenly an officer
emerged from the house, removed his hat, and wiped his
forehead three times with a handkerchief. No one else
noticed, but Henry Wing was in his saddle in seconds, heading for the nearest telegraph office. Thanks to his quick
thinking, the *Tribune* became the first paper in the country
to print the news of the surrender at Appomattox Courthouse. A day later, Henry Wing was on his way to Litchfield,
Connecticut, and his job as an editor.

The first issue published by the *Enquirer's* new owner
appeared on April 15, 1865. Ironically, the headlines bore
the sad news that the president of the United States had
been assassinated at Ford's Theater the night before.

In later years, Henry Wing sold his interest in the Litchfield *Enquirer* and followed his father's footsteps into the
ministry. He died in 1925 at the age of eighty-five, treasuring
until the end of his life the memory of his brief friendship
with Abraham Lincoln and remembering especially the night
the president kissed his cheek.

4

Januarius Aloysius MacGahan

In the summer of 1884, a navy cruiser, the U.S.S. *Powhatan,* steamed home from Europe with the remains of an American war correspondent in its hold. The ship, flag at half-mast, docked in New York Harbor, and a guard of honor escorted the journalist's casket down to City Hall. After a brief ceremony there, the body was taken to Ohio and laid to rest on a peaceful hillside not far from the town of New Lexington in Perry County.

The man who was honored with this unusual tribute was Januarius Aloysius MacGahan—an audacious and irrepressible reporter for the *New York Herald.* A six-foot-three-inch giant, MacGahan sported a black moustache and beard and was rarely without his riding boots and Astrakhan cap. But despite his flamboyant appearance, the Cossack Correspondent, as he was called, was a top-notch reporter—daring, persistent, and dedicated to the truth.

MacGahan was born near New Lexington, Ohio, in 1844. His parents were Irish immigrants who had left a small and unprofitable farm in the Old World for a larger and richer one in the New. The elder MacGahan never ceased to curse the English landlords who had driven him from his native country. He died when Januarius was only seven, leaving his son two things—his hatred of oppression and his Irish gift for words.

Whether he chose to talk or to write, Januarius Aloysius MacGahan was a born storyteller. He had, in addition, a talent for languages and had taught himself to speak both French and German fluently. Along with his other verbal abilities, MacGahan was remarkably persuasive. At the age of twenty-four, without any previous newspaper experience, he managed to talk himself into a job as special European correspondent for the *New York Herald*.

MacGahan's first scoop was a series of personal interviews with some of the most prominent men in Europe. On top of that, in 1870 he succeeded in being one of the first correspondents to arrive in Paris at the end of the Franco-Prussian War. The city was in the throes of a bitter revolt, with the working classes literally up in arms against the National Assembly's acceptance of the treaty with Prussia. They had set up their own government, known as the Commune, and controlled most of Paris. The *Herald* staff man was the only reporter behind the workers' barricades. When the revolt collapsed MacGahan was hurled into prison, and only the intervention of the American ambassador saved him from being executed with the other Communards.

After the Franco-Prussian War, MacGahan roamed about Europe, finally turning up in Russia in 1873 as a guest of Czar Alexander II at his summer palace on the Black Sea. The Russian court was suspicious of outsiders and Americans were particularly unwelcome. But Januarius MacGahan charmed his hosts with hair-raising tales of his narrow escapes in the Paris Commune and various other stories of his travels through Europe.

One day, while hiking along a rocky hillside, the reporter fell and broke a bone in his foot. He was immediately placed in one of the most comfortable rooms in the palace, and for the next three weeks most of the Russian court could be found at his bedside listening to his fund of witty stories. When the czar left the Black Sea retreat to return to the winter palace in Saint Petersburg (now Leningrad), Mac-Gahan was invited to come along.

Not long after his arrival in the Russian capital, the American correspondent learned that the czar was sending an army into Central Asia. The objective was Khiva, a Moslem kingdom near the Chinese border. Capturing the remote and supposedly impregnable state would not only extend Russia's territory farther eastward, but would also establish her reputation as a first-class military power.

The czar had decreed that no foreigners were to accompany the expedition to Khiva. MacGahan coolly ignored the order. He quietly arranged to hire a pair of servants and several horses, and set off to join the action.

The distance from Saint Petersburg to Khiva was more than thirty-five hundred miles. There was no road and the terrain was treacherous; first there were frozen Siberian wastelands, then endless stretches of sunbaked desert. The only people to be found along the way were nomadic tribesmen who were not noted for extending hospitality to wandering strangers.

"Being a man of peace," Januarius MacGahan wrote, "I went but lightly armed. . . . A heavy double-barreled English hunting rifle, a double-barreled shotgun . . . an eighteen-shooter Winchester rifle, three heavy revolvers, and one ordinary muzzle-loading shotgun . . . besides a few knives and sabres, formed a light and unpretentious equipment."

"Nothing was farther from my thoughts than fighting," he added. "I only encumbered myself with these things in order to be able to discuss with becoming dignity questions relating to the rights of way and of property with inhabitants of the desert, whose opinions on these subjects are sometimes peculiar."

As it turned out, MacGahan had little need for his arsenal. When he came to a settlement he would enter one of the tents, toss his holster and revolver to the owner, and throw himself down before the fire. The gesture, indicating that he was a man of peace, worked. He rarely had trouble finding food and shelter for the night.

As MacGahan's journey continued, however, settlements became harder and harder to find. He had to rely on wild sheep for his food, and at one point he was without water for twenty-four hours. When he finally came to a pool it was only a shallow patch of mud, but the parched traveler buried his face in the slime and gratefully lapped up whatever moisture he could find.

MacGahan had left Saint Petersburg with only his servants for company, but he hoped to overtake the Russian army commanded by General Kaufmann. Kaufmann's troops, however, had taken a different route and MacGahan was forced to make the entire journey alone.

The trip across the desert might have been less harrowing if he had been able to procure a camel train, but none was available and he was forced to rely on horses. The sand drifts were often piled as high as twenty-five or thirty feet, and the animals sank in right up to their bellies. Two of the horses collapsed and died from exhaustion, but Mac-Gahan pushed relentlessly on.

After almost two weeks of struggling through shifting sands and scorching sun, he finally emerged from the desert. Now there was a new enemy. The tribesmen who inhabited this section of the continent were far more ferocious than the nomads. MacGahan had seen pictures of Turkoman warriors riding off with sacks full of their enemy's heads, so whenever he stopped for the night he or one of his servants stood guard by the camp fire.

To their relief, no Turkomans showed up. MacGahan realized that they were busy elsewhere when he awoke one morning to the boom of cannon fire. General Kaufmann's army was less than a mile away and was already launching an attack against Khiva.

MacGahan rushed to the battlefield, but discovered to his horror that he was approaching it from the enemy side. There was one small opening in the Turkoman lines. The correspondent galloped through at breakneck speed, tore across the no-man's-land that separated the two armies, and pulled up in front of a Russian sentry on the other side.

"*Vui kto?* Who are you?" said the astonished soldier.

"*Americanetz*," MacGahan replied.

When the sentry brought him to his regimental commander and MacGahan explained how he had gotten there, the officer shook his head in disbelief. "*Molodyetz*—brave fellow," was all he could say.

The Russian officer invited the reporter to breakfast and questioned him further about his journey. MacGahan had been ridiculously foolhardy, the general and his staff agreed. His chances of surviving such a dangerous expedition had been about a hundred to one. The officer then proceeded to give the newspaperman such a frightening account of the dangers he had escaped that, said MacGahan, "I experienced something of the feeling of the man who, having killed, as he supposed, a fine large wolf, was aghast upon being told he had slain the largest and most magnificent lioness that had ever been seen in the country."

MacGahan had made his incredible trip into Asia completely unaware that he was being pursued by a small army of Cossacks with orders to arrest him. He had violated the czar's rule against foreign travelers accompanying the expedition. The Cossacks were noted for being indefatigable horsemen, but they had no luck keeping up with the American newsman. Several times they almost turned back, convinced that MacGahan could not possibly survive in the desert and had probably been devoured by jackals. When at last they rode into General Kaufmann's headquarters and found Januarius Aloysius MacGahan alive and well, the Cossacks not only agreed that he was *molodyetz,* but they even let him talk them out of arresting him. As MacGahan pointed out, the czar's order had mentioned only Europeans, and he was an American.

The battle for Khiva promised to be a bitter one. Five times Russian troops had tried to invade the kingdom. They had been driven back each time. Once a detachment almost succeeded in capturing the capital city, but the Turkomans won it back and slaughtered their would-be conquerors to the last man. This time, however, after one brief battle—the one in which MacGahan had ridden through the enemy lines—the khan who ruled Khiva agreed to a surrender.

General Kaufmann's forces, MacGahan with them, marched peacefully into the capital. The city with its mosques and minarets and marble palace presented a picture right out of a story book. The newspaperman, one of the first Americans to view it, was enchanted with what he saw.

The Khivan men all had long black beards, and over their cotton shirts and loose trousers they wore a khalat, a long straight-cut tunic reaching to their heels. Their feet were bare, but on their heads they wore enormous black caps that weighed six or seven pounds. "The heavy sheepskin cap alone is enough to destroy the working of the most active brain," MacGahan commented wryly, "and upon seeing their monstrous hats, I no longer wondered at the backward state of their civilization."

The reporter was granted an interview with the khan, who offered him tea and melons. The ruler thought his guest was English. When he discovered that MacGahan was from America, he demanded to know if that was near England. "No," the reporter told him, "my country is much farther away."

"How far?"

"It is away over a great sea four hundred days' march of a camel."

The khan could not imagine how the American had crossed such an enormous sea. MacGahan told him about the steamboat that could travel forty times as fast as a camel and the telegraph that could send a message from Yalta to Saint Petersburg in a matter of minutes.

"This statement appeared to him too amazing to be believed," MacGahan reported, "and I think he looked on me as a great liar."

For a while after the march on Khiva, Januarius Aloysius MacGahan's adventures were comparatively tame. He joined an American naval squadron in the Mediterranean for a trip to Cuba. Then he returned to London to write a book about his experiences in Central Asia. The following summer he went to Spain, where a civil war was raging between the people who favored the king—the Carlists—and those who opposed him—the Republicans. At times, the only way the two opposing forces could recognize each other was by their hats—fat muffin-shaped caps called *boinas*. The Republicans wore red *boinas*, the Carlists blue. The correspondents who covered the Carlist War generally traveled with one of each, making it easy to switch sides in an emergency.

MacGahan, who favored the Carlists, refused to wear anything but a blue *boina*. His loyalty resulted in his capture by the Republicans, and once more the American foreign service had to come to his rescue. Only the quick action of the United States consul saved him from facing a firing squad.

By the time the Cossack Correspondent returned to England, still another war was brewing in Europe. The Turks, who had conquered Bulgaria in the fourteenth century, were reported to have repressed a nationalist uprising by destroying a number of villages and killing the inhabitants. The story appeared in the *London Daily News* in June, 1876. The Turkish government promptly denied it and Britain's prime minister, Benjamin Disraeli, denounced the *Daily News* for printing sensationalist nonsense.

The editor, Sir John R. Robinson, was outraged at the charge. "To us, at all events, our duty was clear," he said. "We must have a special inquiry into the conditions and the facts—an inquiry to be conducted on the very spot—by a man who would explore the whole scene of the struggle and the controversy—a man of courage and daring, who would make his way under whatever difficulties in each spot—a man of cool head and steady eye, who would see and judge for himself and tell the impartial truth. We found the man in Mr. J. A. MacGahan."

MacGahan readily accepted Sir John's invitation to verify the *Daily News*'s story of what soon became known as "the Bulgarian atrocities." He was the perfect man for the job. Not only did he have a "cool head and steady eye," but by now he had added Russian, Turkish, and several Slavic dialects to his repertory of languages.

MacGahan headed straight for Philippopolis (now Plovdiv), the center of the area where the Turks were supposed to have staged their reprisals. He found the stories substantiated by everyone he met, including the Turks themselves. He also found the burned villages and examined for himself the skeletons of the victims. The first report of his findings went back to the *Daily News*.

"The atrocities admitted on all hands by those friendly to the Turks, and by the Turks themselves, are enough and more than enough. I do not care to go on heaping up the mournful count. When you are met in the outset of your investigation with the admission that sixty or seventy villages have been burned; that some 15,000 people have been slaughtered, of whom a large part were women and children, you begin to feel that it is useless to go any further."

Nevertheless, MacGahan did go further. He sent back almost a dozen dispatches describing the events in Bulgaria. The stories caused a sensation all over Europe. Because Disraeli supported Turkey, MacGahan's accounts of Turkish atrocities played a part in the prime minister's ultimate fall from power. When Russia went to war in April, 1877, to drive her longtime enemy, Turkey, out of Europe and give Bulgaria her independence, MacGahan covered the conflict from the Russian side for both the *London Daily News* and the *New York Herald*.

It proved to be a painful assignment. Shortly before the war, he had broken a bone in his ankle while trying to tame a wild horse. Then, on his first day in the field, with the leg still in a cast, MacGahan's horse stumbled and the correspondent fell over the edge of a precipice. The same bone was broken again. Almost any other newspaperman would have given up and gone home, but MacGahan only shrugged and cheerfully declared that he had never cared much for walking anyhow, so now he would ride all the time.

He had himself lifted onto a gun carriage and continued to advance with the Russian troops. Later he found a transport wagon, but its wheels slipped on a mountain road, injuring MacGahan's leg once again. By now he was almost completely disabled. After a brief rest behind the lines, however, he insisted on returning to the front to cover the final siege at Pleven.

His fellow correspondent on the *Herald*, Frank D. Millet, described MacGahan's devotion to duty. "Half the time at Plevna [Pleven] he was on his back unable to rise. During a battle he would pull himself together and face the bullets and the certain danger of exposure to the weather with cheerfulness and even gayety, for his heart was all in his work."

MacGahan's description of the last battle—"hand to hand, man to man, bayonet to bayonet"—was especially powerful. "The uproar of the battle rose and swelled until it became fearful to hear," he said, "like the continuous roar of an angry sea beating against a rockbound coast, combined with that of a thunder-storm with the strange unearthly noises heard on board a ship when laboring in a gale. . . ."

The Cossack Correspondent stayed up all night to finish his story of the battle. Then he set off to reach the telegraph office at Bucharest. He was riding his favorite horse, a small Turkish animal that followed him about like a pet lamb, and carrying the dispatch in his saddlebags. When he came to the Danube River, he was stopped by the local Russian commandant, who wanted to hear the latest news from Pleven. Tying his horse at the bridge, MacGahan went up to the commandant's hut to give him a report of the victory. When he returned five minutes later, his horse had been stolen. The correspondent, with his bad leg, not only had to walk the rest of the way to Bucharest, but when he got there had to sit down in the telegraph office and completely rewrite his account of the battle.

The Treaty of San Stefano in 1878 ended the bloody Russo-Turkish War and gave Bulgaria its independence, although Russian troops occupied the country for a few years. By then Januarius Aloysius MacGahan had become a national hero. When he rode through their villages, Bulgarian peasants rushed out to kiss his hands. His statue was erected in the public square in Sofia, and for a while there was even talk of electing him prime minister.

Januarius MacGahan's assignment to cover the Russo-Turkish War had given him an opportunity to renew his friendship with a Russian officer he had met some years before in the war against Khiva—Mikhail Dmitrievich Skobelev.

Skobelev, like MacGahan, stood over six feet tall. Like the correspondent, too, he was completely fearless. "He always wore a white coat, a white hat, and rode a white horse in battle, simply because other generals usually avoided these target-marks," wrote one man who knew him. "He never lost an opportunity of displaying courage. . . . Yet all this was not mere bravado and nonsense, but was the result of almost cold-blooded calculation. It was intended to impress his men and it did so. They firmly believed he could not be hit."

MacGahan and Skobelev often went riding and took their meals together. They also enjoyed insulting each other. MacGahan was always singing. His fellow correspondents used to complain that his ditties woke them up in the morning and chased them to bed at night. Skobelev had heard MacGahan's music in Khiva. When they met again in Bulgaria, the Russian swore that MacGahan had not learned anything since they were together in the desert—"except some new bits of song that are more abominably stupid than the old ones."

The Cossack Correspondent remained in Constantinople for some months after the Russo-Turkish War. Early in June one of his American friends, an army engineer named Francis Vinton Greene, fell ill of typhoid. MacGahan insisted on nursing the young officer back to health. Two days later, the reporter himself fell ill. The fever attacked his brain and he died in convulsions at the end of a week, only a few days before his thirty-fourth birthday.

Januarius Aloysius MacGahan was buried in a small Greek cemetery on June 11, 1878. Representatives from both the American and Russian embassies attended the funeral, and his fellow newspapermen served as pallbearers. Mac-Gahan's old friend Skobelev was also among the mourners. When the correspondent's casket was lowered into its grave, the Russian general broke down and sobbed like a child.

He was a legend in his own lifetime, and Januarius Aloysius MacGahan's fame continued even after his premature death. For years masses for the repose of his soul were said annually in all the churches of Bulgaria. On the other side of the Atlantic, the Ohio legislature voted in 1884 to have the state's distinguished son brought home. And in New York City, over a thousand attended a memorial service at City Hall.

MacGahan's courage captured his readers' imagination; his honesty earned their respect. "No man of his age in recent years has done more to bring honor on the name of America throughout the length and breadth of Europe and far into Asia," said his friend Francis Vinton Greene. "No man has more faithfully served the English-speaking races by telling them the truth about great events in attractive form in their daily papers."

5

Winston Churchill

TWENTY-FIVE POUNDS REWARD—
DEAD OR ALIVE
Englishman, twenty-five years old, about five feet
eight inches high, indifferent build, walks a little with
a bend forward, pale appearance, red-brownish hair,
small moustache hardly perceptible, talks through his
nose, cannot pronounce the letter S properly and does
not know any Dutch.

The fugitive described so unflatteringly on this "wanted"
poster was to become one of the outstanding statesmen of
the twentieth century. But at the time, Winston Churchill
was better known as a war correspondent for the *London
Morning Post*.

The future prime minister of Great Britain was the son of
Lord Randolph Churchill, leader of the House of Commons,
and his beautiful American-born wife, Jennie Jerome. Young
Winston was educated at Harrow and the royal Military
College at Sandhurst. Churchill once remarked that he had
been sent to Sandhurst because his father thought he wasn't
bright enough to study law. Quite possibly he was right.

Winston had no talent for Latin, French, or mathematics. In fact, the only subject in which he excelled was English. All through school, he was far and away the best writer in his class.

At Sandhurst, however, Churchill discovered that he also had a gift for military studies. When he graduated in 1894 and was commissioned a subaltern in the British army, he began looking for a chance to put his newly developed skills to work. There had been no lack of wars in the past; there would be none in the future. But at that particular point in Queen Victoria's reign, Great Britain seemed at peace with the entire world.

Spain, however, had recently sent a large force to Cuba to subdue a guerrilla army that was fighting for that colony's independence. So the recently commissioned officer arranged to spend his two-and-a-half-month winter leave as a member of the Spanish army. Although Churchill's service in Cuba was brief, it provided him with what he called a "private rehearsal" for being under fire. It also launched his career as a journalist. To help pay his expenses, he secured an assignment from the *London Daily Graphic* to write a series of newspaper articles about the rebellion against Spain.

When his winter leave was up, Churchill returned to London and discovered that his regiment was being ordered to India. Its garrison was at Bangalore, a picturesque but quiet city where the subaltern did little soldiering and still less news reporting. Reading and playing polo became his principal pastimes.

In 1897, while Churchill was home on leave, a religious leader known as the "Mad Mullah" organized a revolt in the north of India and attacked the British regiments stationed at Malakand Pass. Three brigades were immediately ordered to the frontier. They were commanded by Sir Bindon Blood,

already renowned as the most experienced English officer
in India. Winston Churchill had met General Blood at Deepdene, the country estate of his aunt and uncle. The old
officer and the young one had taken an immediate liking to
each other. "On Sunday morning on the sunny lawns of
Deepdene," Churchill recounted, "I extracted from the general a promise that if ever he commanded another expedition on the Indian frontier, he would let me come with him."

The instant he learned that Sir Bindon Blood was to command the Malakand Field Force, Winston Churchill fired
off a telegram reminding him of his promise. Simultaneously,
he began making arrangements to return to India. It was
a long, hot voyage, made even more unpleasant by Sir Bindon Blood's failure to reply to his telegram. It was not until
Churchill reached Bombay that one of the ship's officers
finally handed him the return wire. "Very difficult: no
vacancies," it read. "Come up as a correspondent; will try to
fit you in. B. B."

Churchill lost no time in making the necessary arrangements. "Having realized that if a British cavalry officer waits
until he is ordered on active service, he is likely to wait a
considerable time," he wrote later, "I obtained six weeks
leave of absence from my regiment, and on September 2, arrived in Malakand as press correspondent of the *Pioneer* and
Daily Telegraph, and in the hope of sooner or later being
attached to the force in a military capacity."

The soldier-journalist at last found a little of the excitement he had missed in his leisurely tour of duty at Bangalore. He made a nerve-racking march across a slender rope
bridge swinging over a yawning crevice, visited the strong-
holds of the local khans, and, climbing to the top of a craggy
pass, gazed down on "a valley upon which perhaps no white

man had looked since Alexander crossed the mountains on his way to India."

Churchill made arrangements with friendly tribesmen in the area to carry his reports of the expedition back to the nearest telegraph office at Panjkora. The Mad Mullah's followers occupied twenty miles of countryside along the way, but the messengers never had any trouble getting through. In fact, on more than one occasion Churchill's wires arrived in London before the official dispatches to the War Office.

Sir Bindon Blood's suppression of the Indian uprising proved to be a quick and fairly peaceful operation, but Churchill's experiences with the Malakand Field Force whetted his appetite for further adventure. When another field force, under Sir William Lockhart, was sent to Tirah to quell a second revolt of Indian tribesmen, he tried desperately to have himself assigned to it. He was told that there were enough officers in the field force. The only way he could get to Tirah was to become a member of Lockhart's personal staff. Since Churchill did not even know the general, his chances appeared hopeless. But he had no intention of giving up.

When the regimental polo team from Bangalore went north to play in a tournament, Churchill went along. Meerut, the site of the match, was only six hundred miles from the front. After the game, Churchill—at the risk of being absent without leave—boarded a train for Tirah. His plan was to go directly to Sir William Lockhart and present his request in person.

The general was busy, but his aide-de-camp, Captain Haldane, agreed to see the unexpected visitor. Winston Churchill talked fast and furiously for half an hour. When he had finished, Haldane excused himself to go see the commander in chief. He returned in a few minutes with the news that Sir William Lockhart had decided to appoint the glib young officer to his personal staff.

Although the assignment provided Churchill with a series of fascinating news stories, it did little to advance his military career. The dispute with the Indian tribesmen was settled by negotiation and the Tirah Expeditionary Force was soon demobilized.

Winston Churchill was again home on leave when the War Office announced the organization of still another British force. Sir Herbert Kitchener was being sent to the Egyptian Sudan to recapture Khartoum. The former British city was in the hands of Mohammed Ahmed, leader of a native religious sect whose members were known as dervishes.

Churchill was determined to get a place on Kitchener's staff. He prevailed on his mother to write a personal letter to the general, whom she knew fairly well. Kitchener's reply was a polite but firm no.

Churchill next took his appeal to the prime minister, Lord Salisbury. The journalist had written a military history of the Malakand Field Force that had come to Lord Salisbury's attention. The prime minister had summoned Churchill to his office, praised his work lavishly, and spent almost a half hour talking to him about the expedition. If there was anything he could do to help him, Lord Salisbury had said as he was leaving, Churchill was not to hesitate to call upon him.

Churchill debated for some days whether to ask Salisbury to intercede for him with Kitchener. He decided to go ahead when it became evident that, if he did not get to the Sudan soon, the fighting would be over. Although the prime minister agreed to wire Kitchener about Churchill, he couched

A cartoon from England's satirical magazine *Punch* showing
William Howard Russell reporting on a battle.

The Granger Collection

George Washburn Smalley.

Culver Pictures

A portrait of Henry Wing as a war correspondent.

Januarius Aloysius MacGahan.

Winston Spencer Churchill in the uniform of the South African
Light Horse during the Boer War.

James Creelman in his field clothes.

Richard Harding Davis in uniform.

Floyd Gibbons after losing his left eye in the Battle of
Belleau Wood during World War I.

Ernie Pyle sets up his typewriter in the middle of a field
in Normandy during World War II.

Marguerite Higgins in Tokyo during the Korean War.

the request in terms that left the final choice up to the general. Back came another no. Kitchener already had all the officers he required.

Undaunted, Churchill sought out the supreme commander of the British army, Sir Evelyn Wood. As a result, the prime minister's request became an order and Winston Churchill was named a lieutenant of the Twenty-first Lancers. He would have no specific duties and he would have to pay all his own expenses. Churchill was satisfied. He already had an assignment to write a series of letters about the campaign for the *Morning Post*. The salary would more than cover his passage to Egypt.

The decisive battle of the Sudan campaign was fought at Omdurman. It marked the end of dervish power and made Lord Kitchener a military hero. It also gave Winston Churchill his first real taste of war.

The Twenty-first Lancers were among the twenty-six thousand British troops ordered to advance against fifty-five thousand dervishes. Churchill rode straight through a long, galloping line of screaming enemy troops, their deadly cutlasses gleaming in the sunlight. Soldiers on either side of him were killed, but the lieutenant charged right through the dervish lines, escaping one saber blow by inches and saving himself from certain death by drawing his pistol and shooting another man whose sword was raised less than three feet from his head. Of the 310 men of the Twenty-first Lancers, seventy were killed in less than five minutes. Many of those who survived the charge lost their horses, and almost all had their saddles or reins slashed and their clothing shredded by saber thrusts. Churchill emerged unscathed.

The correspondent's description of the cavalry charge caused considerable excitement when it appeared in the

Morning Post. It was not often that the sound and fury of war were captured by a man who had actually been engaged in the fighting.

Despite his proficiency with both pen and sword, Winston Churchill did not plan to remain either a soldier or a journalist for very long. His ultimate ambition was to follow his father's footsteps in Parliament. After the Sudan campaign, he resigned from the army and decided to take his first crack at politics. He stood for a seat in the House of Commons from the district of Oldham and was soundly defeated.

When the would-be politician decided to return to his career as a journalist, there was no need for him to pound the pavements in search of work. In October, 1899, a group of Dutch settlers—the Boers—declared war against the British army that had been sent to protect English lives and property in South Africa. News of the fighting had scarcely reached London when the editor of the *Morning Post* offered Churchill a job as the newspaper's chief correspondent in the war zone. All his expenses would be paid and the salary was 250 pounds a month—over 300 hundred dollars a week. Forty-eight hours later, the ex-soldier was once again on his way to war.

In his efforts to get to the front, Churchill found himself delayed at a town called Estcourt. It was held by the English, but how long it would remain that way was anybody's guess. The enemy had already moved in behind General Ian Hamilton's troops at the front and the city seemed likely to be attacked at any moment. Several troops of British soldiers were garrisoned in Estcourt. General Hamilton decided they were needed at the front and sent an armored train to bring them forward through the Boer lines.

By coincidence, the officer in charge of the train was Captain Haldane, the same man who had interceded for Churchill with Sir William Lockhart at Tirah. Haldane invited his old friend to join him on the trip. It would be a risky journey, as Churchill well knew, but it would also provide some lively copy for his letters to the *Morning Post.*

The troop train departed from Estcourt at dawn on November 15. It reached the first station on the line with no difficulty, and Haldane stopped to wire General Hamilton that the soldiers were on their way. Suddenly a group of figures appeared in the distance. They looked like Boers, and they seemed to be doing something to the rail line. When the train started moving again, the British found out what.

The Boers had rolled a huge boulder onto the railroad tracks just around a curve. Unable to see it, the engineer rounded the bend at high speed and smashed head on into the rock. The impact sent three cars hurtling off the track. As if that wasn't bad enough, the last of the three lay sprawled right across the ties, blocking all further movement along the line.

The wrecked train was in a valley less than a thousand yards from enemy territory. In seconds, the adjacent hills were dotted with Boers, their rifles trained on the hapless survivors of the wreckage below. While Haldane organized his forces to ward off the Dutch riflemen, Churchill decided to see if he could do anything about getting the train started again.

Fortunately, the engine and tender had been at the rear of the cars and had not suffered any damage. If the one car that blocked the tracks could be pushed out of the way, the rest of the train could go through with no difficulty.

Churchill rounded up a party of volunteers and, dodging enemy bullets while they worked, they finally managed to move the overturned railway car partway off the tracks. But they soon discovered that they had not moved it far enough. There was enough room for the undamaged cars to squeeze by, but the engine was somewhat wider. The scant six inches of metal that still protruded over the rails blocked its way.

Unfortunately, the overturned car was jammed in such a position that the more Churchill and his co-workers tried to push it, the worse it got. The only hope was to back up the engine and then drive it ahead full force through the debris, trusting it could push the wreckage aside. The plan worked, but before the Englishmen could couple the other cars back onto the engine, they found themselves surrounded by horsemen.

Winston Churchill had been so absorbed in moving the wrecked train that at first he did not recognize the riders in their slouch hats and dark clothes as Boers. It was not until they raised their rifles that he realized he was in trouble. The bullets missed him by inches. He dashed for cover in a small ravine to one side of the railroad tracks, but another horseman soon loomed in front of him, his rifle at the ready.

Despite his correspondent status, Churchill had decided to carry a pistol. He reached for it now, but the gun wasn't there. It had slipped out of his belt while he was trying to clear the rail line. Alone and unarmed, he found himself face to face with the sinister muzzle of a gun. "Death stood before me, grim and sullen," he wrote later, "Death without his lighthearted companion, Chance."

Remembering Napoleon's words, "When one is alone and unarmed, a surrender may be pardoned," Winston Churchill threw up his hands and allowed himself to be captured as a prisoner of war. As an unarmed civilian, he assumed that he would soon be released. Then he remembered that he was still carrying the clips of ammunition for his missing pistol.

His captors would show him no mercy if they found those, he thought. Slipping one clip hastily out of his pocket, he dropped it to the ground. He was just getting the second out when one of the Boers said sharply, "What have you got there?"

Opening the palm of his hand, Churchill feigned innocence. "What is it?" he said in a puzzed tone. "I picked it up."

The man threw the ammunition clip away and led him off with the other prisoners.

When the Boer officers examined their captives' papers and discovered that one man was the son of one of England's most prominent politicians, they decided that, correspondent or not, he would have to remain in prison. "We are not going to let you go, old chappie," one of the Dutchmen said. "We don't catch the son of a lord every day."

Churchill was taken to Pretoria, the capital of the Boer republic of Transvaal, and imprisoned in the State Model Schools Building, along with several dozen British officers.

For the next three weeks, the captured correspondent conducted a long and fruitless argument with the Boer authorities. Churchill maintained that he should be released because he was a member of the press. The Boers would not hear of it. As the son of Lord Randolph Churchill, he was their prize prisoner. Moreover, he had jeopardized his status as a noncombatant by trying to free the armored train. He was now considered an official prisoner of war.

After three weeks in prison, Churchill decided he had had enough. Sneaking past the sentries under cover of darkness, he scaled a wall and escaped into the garden of a villa next door to the school building. The residents of the villa were having a party and the guests were continually wandering back and forth in the garden. Churchill took cover behind a clump of bushes only a few feet away from them.

While he was still crouched in the shrubbery, an officer who had hoped to escape with him sidled up on the other side of the wall. The sentries suspected he was missing, the man whispered; he'd better climb back right away.

Churchill examined the wall and saw at once that it would be impossible to get back. There was no foothold on the villa side. "Fate pointed onwards," he wrote later. "Besides, I said to myself, 'Of course, I shall be recaptured, but I will at least have a run for the money.'"

In the course of freeing the wrecked train, the newsman had lost his hat. One of his captors had kindly, and innocently, provided him with a replacement—a large, floppy Boer-style hat. Churchill now clapped it jauntily on his head, strolled casually out of the garden, and set off down the road. The streets were full of people, but no one paid any attention to him. When he got to the deserted outskirts of Pretoria, he sat down on the side of the road to decide what to do next.

He had four bars of chocolate and seventy-five pounds in English money. He spoke no Dutch and had no map, but he knew that the shortest route to freedom was a three-hundred-mile trek across the border to Portuguese East Africa. Churchill decided to navigate by the stars. He came to a railroad track that, as far as he could tell, headed toward the Portuguese colony. He followed it, ducking past sentries along the way but otherwise taking no special precautions. "Perhaps that was the reason I succeeded," he wrote later.

A three-hundred-mile hike was out of the question. The next time a train came by, Churchill grabbed onto a car and swung himself aboard. The car was loaded with coal sacks. He promptly buried himself in the middle of them and fell sound asleep. When he awoke at dawn, hungry and parched, he hopped off the train and hid in the woods, eating some of his chocolate and finding a pool from which to quench his thirst.

By now the Boers were scouring the landscape looking for their missing prisoner. The unflattering "wanted" poster, with its offer of a twenty-five-pound reward for his recovery, dead or alive, was distributed in every town. Trains going out of the Dutch colonies were halted and searched, suspicious strangers were stopped on the streets and asked to show their papers. Still the elusive newspaper correspondent could not be found. One rumor said he was working as a waiter in Pretoria; another that he was disguised as a woman; still another that he had been shot and killed by Boer sentries.

Winston Churchill spent all day and most of the night in the woods by the railroad tracks. At last he decided to ask for help. If all else failed, the seventy-five pounds in his pocket might buy his way to safety.

The woods were not far from a mining town that Churchill knew had a number of English inhabitants. The only problem was how to tell which house belonged to a Briton and which to a Boer. Never reluctant to take a chance, Churchill simply walked into the village, selected the first house he saw, marched up, and knocked at the door.

When the owner answered, the escaped prisoner explained that he had had an accident and needed help. The man looked skeptical. Churchill glanced at the revolver in his hand and decided to tell the truth. "I am Winston Churchill, war correspondent for the *Morning Post*," he said. "I escaped last night from Pretoria. I am making my way to the frontier. I have plenty of money. Will you help me?"

The man lowered his gun, walked over, and carefully locked the door. "Thank God you have come here," he said. "It is the only house for twenty miles where you would not have been handed over. But we are all British here and we will see you through."

The man was a mineowner named John Howard. He gave his visitor some food and, just before dawn, led him across the yard to the mine shaft. There was a small secret chamber far down in the mine where Churchill could hide until the coast was clear.

Another Englishman operated the elevator that carried him down to the hideout. The man had not only heard all about young Churchill's daring escape, but he was also from Oldham and remembered the correspondent through his unsuccessful campaign for Parliament. "Don't worry," he assured Churchill as he escorted him to his hiding place. "They'll all vote for you next time."

Less than an hour after the reporter had disappeared into the blackness, a Boer search party arrived in town. Howard, being an Englishman, was suspected of hiding the fugitive, but a systematic search of the entire district turned up no trace of the missing prisoner. The Boers finally left to continue their manhunt somewhere else.

As soon as it was safe to let Churchill out, Howard arranged for him to be concealed in a shipment of wool that was being sent to Portuguese East Africa. Churchill was jammed into a narrow space between two bales of wool, but somehow managed to find a small chink between the bundles where he could peer out and watch the train's progress.

There were several stops and a number of delays. At one station he could hear people talking excitedly in Dutch and he was certain that the train was being searched. If it was, nobody bothered to check the freight cars. The next time Churchill looked out through his peephole, he spied the cap of a Portuguese official on the train platform. Pushing his head out into the open, he sang and shouted for joy.

As soon as the train reached its destination, Churchill climbed down from his hiding place and made his way to the British consulate. The minute he mentioned his name, he was given a hearty welcome and provided with a hot bath, clean clothes, and a full-course dinner. He soon learned that the story of his escape was front-page news. The British had suffered several disastrous defeats in South Africa, and the first encouraging report from the front was the news that an intrepid young war correspondent had somehow succeeded in outwitting the Boers. Winston Churchill was a national hero.

On December 21, almost six weeks after his capture, he was able to write back to the *Morning Post*:

"I am very weak, but I am free.

"I have lost many pounds, but I am lighter in heart.

"I shall also avail myself of every opportunity from this moment to urge with earnestness an unflinching and uncompromising prosecution of the war."

Churchill returned to England soon afterward, and before long he was again a candidate for a seat in the House of Commons from Oldham. This time, as the man in the mine shaft had predicted, he was elected by an overwhelming majority.

Winston Churchill's career as a war correspondent was over; his career as a statesman was just beginning. He had no regrets about abandoning journalism. The future for him was clear. "I can never doubt which is the right end to be at," he once said about the choice he had made. "It is better to be making news than taking it."

6

James Creelman

In 1901 James Creelman wrote a book about his adventures as a special correspondent. *On the Great Highway* referred to the highway of life, but it was especially appropriate because Creelman's career in the newspaper business began soon after he set out on a real highway—the long road between Montreal and New York.

James Creelman was born in Montreal on November 12, 1859. His parents separated when he was still quite young, and the boy was left in Canada with his father while his mother moved to New York. One day, not long after his twelfth birthday, James decided to follow her. It was a four-hundred-mile trip and, except for an occasional ride on some farmer's wagon, he walked the entire distance. When James finally arrived at his mother's rooming house, his shoes were worn through to the soles of his feet and, of the hoard of coins he had saved to finance his trip, there was only a lonely nickel left in his pocket.

Martha Creelman was stunned when the dusty traveler appeared on her doorstep, but she happily took him in and promised that he could stay. James had been with his mother less than a week when they had their first disagreement. The boy wanted to go out to work; his mother insisted that he go to school. Mrs. Creelman won the argument, but it was a temporary victory. James was bored with his studies and soon convinced her that they would both benefit if he went out to work—he would escape from the drudgery of the classroom, she would have his earnings to help support them.

Martha Creelman reluctantly agreed. James almost found himself back in school, however, when he came home one day and announced that he had found a job in the printing plant of an Episcopal newspaper. Mrs. Creelman was a staunch Presbyterian. Although the apprentice printer somehow managed to convince his mother that he would be unharmed by the experience, she was much happier when he finally quit to become a reporter on the *Brooklyn Eagle*. From there he moved to the *New York Herald*.

Creelman soon became one of the *Herald*'s star reporters. His specialty was the personal interview. He traveled around the world talking to kings and princes, and even arranged an audience with Pope Leo XIII—the first time a pontiff had ever granted an interview to a newspaperman.

Creelman became angry at the *Herald* when its publisher, James Gordon Bennett, decided he could no longer have a by-line on his stories. Bennett thought all interviews that appeared in the paper should be published anonymously. Creelman disagreed and in 1894 stalked off to join the staff of one of the *Herald*'s rivals, the *New York World*. He was immediately assigned to cover the war between China and Japan over which country would control Korea.

At times the Sino-Japanese War resembled a comic opera. The Chinese army still followed the old custom of sending out a cow and a band of trumpeters to announce the beginning of a battle. At the storming of Pyongyang, Korea, which

Creelman witnessed, they decorated the city's walls with hundreds of crimson and yellow banners, including an immense flag for each of the six Chinese generals, in sizes according to their rank.

The battle was still in progress when gray clouds abruptly appeared in the sky and it began to rain. The Chinese soldiers quickly put up oiled-paper umbrellas to keep them dry while they fought. "In every direction," Creelman reported, "Chinese umbrellas could be seen, glistening like turtles on the earthworks."

The untrained Chinese were no match for Japan's up-to-date army, and they soon hoisted the white flag of surrender. When a party of Japanese officers approached the city to discuss the terms, however, the Chinese generals informed them quite seriously that they couldn't surrender in the rain. They suggested calling off the battle until the following day. They would surrender when the weather cleared.

The Japanese declined and returned to their lines to continue the assault. That night, the Chinese abandoned the city and withdrew into Manchuria. At dawn the Japanese marched into Pyongyang. "That victory," said Creelman, "ended the power of China in Korea."

James Creelman once described how he wrote the story of the storming of Pyongyang:

"Lying on the parched grass at night, with my cracked lantern tied to an ancient arrow stuck in the ground, the breeze fluttering the clumsy sheets of native paper on which I set down the details of this historic struggle, I could hear the jolly whistling of my blanket comrade, Frederic Villiers, the famous war artist, as he worked on his pictures in a wrecked pagoda two hundred feet away."

When the dispatch was finished, Creelman's next problem was to get it back to the *New York World.* He took a junk down the Tai-Tong (now the Daido) River, then a steamer along the Korean coast to Chemulpo (now Inchon). From there a messenger took his dispatch by boat to Japan, where it could be cabled to San Francisco and then telegraphed across the continent to New York City.

Despite the sometimes ridiculous behavior of the Chinese army, the battle of Pyongyang was more awful than amusing. By the time Creelman arrived at the tiny seaport of Chemulpo, he was feeling sick and discouraged from the bloodshed he had just witnessed. Then, having so recently been surrounded by death, he was abruptly reminded of life. A messenger at the steamship landing handed him a cable from home. It contained two words: "BOY—WELL."

The message was the announcement of the birth of James Creelman's first child. It bore the seals of thirteen different army headquarters, showing how far the good news had traveled before it finally reached him.

On his way back to Pyongyang that night, the correspondent spied the Japanese fleet, which had just dropped anchor at the mouth of the Tai-Tong River. Only hours before, the force had defeated the Chinese in the battle of the Yalu—one of the first naval encounters in which modern warships were used. No other newsman had the story.

The delighted Creelman hailed the fleet's flagship and was promptly taken aboard. Admiral Ito, the commanding officer, was asleep, but he arose, greeted the correspondent warmly, and even sent for his fleet officers to provide further details about the battle. It was a major news story, and when Creelman had finished quizzing the assembled naval officers Admiral Ito turned to him.

"It is a big piece of news for you," he said.

"Yes," the correspondent answered, "but I have received a still greater piece of news."

Creelman took out the cable announcing the birth of his son and read it aloud. Admiral Ito insisted that they celebrate the event with a bottle of champagne. Standing in a circle, the admiral and his officers clinked their glasses together and drank to the health of a little American boy thousands of miles away.

After the conquest of Korea, the next Japanese target was Manchuria. Creelman rode with the invading army, subsisting on the soldiers' meager rations of dried peas and water. When they reached the city of Kinchow and captured it without a struggle, the tired and hungry newsman made his headquarters in a shop along one of the main streets. His bed was a heap of embroidered silks, his pillow a brightly painted Oriental wood carving. "It was like fairyland to awaken in such a scene of shimmering splendor," he said. "But I must confess that the most glorious thing in that room was a plain tin of Chicago corned beef. Such is the coarse nature of a war correspondent after a forced march on dried peas and water."

The next Japanese objective was Port Arthur. The Chinese garrison withdrew after a brief battle, but when the conquering army marched into the city, they found the bodies of Japanese dead lying on the roadside, headless and horribly multilated.

The enraged Japanese retaliated by killing everyone in the city. The *World* reporter described the wanton massacre with brutal frankness: "Unarmed men, kneeling in the streets and begging for life, were shot, bayoneted, or beheaded. The town was sacked from end to end, and the inhabitants were butchered in their own houses."

Creelman's dispatches inspired cries of outrage from all over the world. The Japanese government denied the incident and accused the reporter of making it up to discredit them. But Creelman refused to retract his story, and, as further proof of its accuracy, produced pictures that had been taken by the English artist and photographer Frederic Villiers.

James Creelman's fearless reporting of the Sino-Japanese War made him famous. He had no sooner returned home from China than the *New York Journal* hired him away from the *World* and sent him to Cuba to cover the revolt that would soon evolve into the Spanish-American War.

The insurrection—and the arrival of eight thousand Spanish troops to put it down—were subjects of great interest in the United States. American newspapers, hungry for headlines, decided to capitalize on the nation's interest. William Randolph Hearst, publisher of the *New York Journal*, went so far as to turn the fight for Cuba's independence into a crusade.

Hearst was overjoyed when his new correspondent's first dispatch from Havana described a brutal execution by the Spaniards of some Cuban prisoners of war. Next, Creelman found the graves of thirty-three Cuban farmers who had been needlessly slaughtered by Spanish troops. His reporting of both incidents so infuriated the Spanish commander in Cuba that Creelman was expelled from the island. But the *Journal* had no trouble finding another war for him to cover.

In 1897 he went to Greece to report on the conflict between that country and Turkey over possession of the island of Crete. While out riding one day, Creelman chanced to cross the narrow boundary between the two enemy armies. He took advantage of the opportunity to conduct an interview with the Turkish field marshal, with a correspondent from a Constantinople newspaper serving as interpreter.

In 1898, after the sinking of the battleship *Maine* in Havana Harbor, America entered the war against Spain. James

Creelman returned to Cuba to report on this new phase of the war. On his first visit to the island, the correspondent had been so disgusted at the things he saw that he had vowed "to help to extinguish Spanish sovereignty in Cuba, if I had to shed my blood for it."

During the Spanish-American War Creelman actually did shed his blood in the dramatic charge at El Caney. The village was one of several objectives along the route to the more important city of Santiago, and a general with whom he was friendly had slipped Creelman the word that it might be the scene of some important fighting. The *Journal* reporter stole away from his fellow correspondents and made his way through sweltering jungles and slimy swamps to the hills just outside El Caney.

He found a spot that offered an excellent view of the Spanish fort. He was so close, in fact, that he could actually see the faces of its defenders. As the battle began Creelman sat silently, pencil in hand, watching the American infantrymen inching their way up the steep hill that led to the fort. The fighting continued for several hours but, although their losses appeared to be heavy, the enemy refused to surrender the fort.

After watching the unsuccessful attack for some time, Creelman made his way from his own vantage point to another ridge where the American commander, General Adna Chaffee, had stationed himself. Bullets were flying all around the general. Before the reporter could even ask Chaffee about the progress of the fighting, one of them glanced across the general's chest, clipping a button from his tunic. Seconds later another bullet ripped the cape from Creelman's raincoat. "Looks better without it," Chaffee remarked drily.

The two men crawled to a safer position under a large

tree. Creelman told the general that he had been studying the fort at close range and, in his opinion, it could be won only by a bayonet charge. He had already observed a "wrinkle" in the hill that would provide cover for an assault party to sneak up unobserved.

Adna Chaffee sent a party of scouts to investigate Creelman's "wrinkle." When they returned with a favorable report, he instructed his adjutant to order F Company to prepare for a charge. Creelman was to lead it.

The correspondent later described the assault: "We pushed our way through a line of low bushes and started up the hill to the fort. The only weapon I had was a revolver, and the holster was slung around to the back so that I should not be tempted to draw.

"When I found myself out on the clear escarped slope, in front of the fort and its deadly trench, walking at the head of a storming party, I began to realize that I had ceased to be a journalist and was now—foolishly or wisely, recklessly, meddlesomely, or patriotically—a part of the army, a soldier without warrant to kill.

"It is only three hundred feet to the top of the hill, and yet the slope looked a mile long."

The Spaniards had erected a barbed wire fence around the trench outside the fort. It had evidently not occurred to them that Yankee soldiers were equipped with wire snippers. When the Americans reached the trench, the captain of F Company called for two soldiers to cut the wires. The Americans swarmed across the trench and into the fort, and the Spaniards quickly raised their hands in surrender.

Creelman was anxious to capture the Spanish flag as a souvenir of the charge, but an American sharpshooter had already sent it fluttering to the ground outside. The reporter rushed out, picked up the red and yellow banner, and waved a victory signal to the rest of the Americans at the bottom of the hill.

The gesture brought sharp bursts of gunfire from another Spanish garrison entrenched on a neighboring hill. Creelman felt a stinging pain and looked down to discover that a bullet had smashed through the upper part of his left arm and had torn a hole in his back.

A detachment of American soldiers carried the wounded newsman down the hill and laid him in the grass with the rest of the wounded. Soon Creelman was delirious with pain and fever. To add to his distress, Spanish bullets were still whizzing overhead. Blurred figures moved back and forth in front of his eyes, and strange voices thundered in his ears; the whole world whirled around him.

Suddenly, out of the mass of strange sounds and shapes, Creelman discerned a familiar figure. "Some one knelt in the grass beside me and put his hand on my fevered head," he wrote. "Opening my eyes, I saw Mr. Hearst, the proprietor of the *New York Journal,* a straw hat with a bright ribbon on his head, a revolver at his belt, and a pencil and notebook in his hand. The man who had provoked the war had come to see the result with his own eyes and, finding one of his correspondents prostrate, was doing the work himself. Slowly he took down my story of the fight. Again and again the tinging of Mauser bullets interrupted. But he seemed unmoved. The battle had to be reported somehow."

While one of his aides found some cool water and a crude bandage for Creelman, William Randolph Hearst took down the story of the charge at El Caney from its leader's own lips. Then, leaving the correspondent to the care of the army doctors, Hearst rode off to find the nearest cable station.

James Creelman's career was by no means ruined by a

bullet in the arm. After his wound healed he went on to cover the important battles against the Spanish in the Philippines. At the end of the war the Philippines became an American possession, and Creelman remained in Manila to wait for an official proclamation outlining the United States' plans for the islands. Even though he had been in the thick of many bloody battles and had been wounded while leading an infantry charge, Creelman later claimed that this peacetime event resulted in the most harrowing adventure of his career—a race with a woman reporter.

The proclamation was considered major news in the United States and every newspaper in the country wanted to be the first to publish it. In fact, one daily was so anxious that its editors had authorized their correspondent to pay up to two thousand dollars for an advance copy of the historic message.

But the United States Commission had no intention of revealing the contents of its proclamation prematurely. All the correspondents in Manila were forced to assemble in the reception room of the commission's headquarters to await the official announcement. Creelman, determined to get his story to the *Journal* first, stationed himself right next to the door. He also ordered his driver to turn his horse and carriage in the direction of the military censor's office where he would have to submit his copy before it could be sent out on the cable.

Surveying the other correspondents in the room, Creelman quickly surmised that his chief rival for a scoop would be a young woman—the wife of a newsman who had been hospitalized with a wound in his foot. The woman also sat near the door, and Creelman saw with alarm that her horse was much stronger than his.

After a few minutes, the president of the United States

Commission for the Philippines appeared in the reception room with several copies of the long-awaited proclamation in his hand. Creelman snatched one, raced to his carriage, and ordered his driver to take off immediately. The astonished president had barely recovered from Creelman's assault when the wounded newsman's wife rushed forward, grabbed another of the printed sheets, and followed Creelman out the door.

It was a furious race. Creelman first offered his driver fifty *pesetas* for victory, then raised the price to a hundred. Finally, as the woman's carriage seemed to be gaining on them, the frantic correspondent called to his driver, "I'll give you the horse if you beat her!"

Creelman was choking from the dust along the road; his body ached from the jolts. As a final indignity, his carriage smashed into a wagon drawn by a water buffalo, and the correspondent was hurled unceremoniously to the ground. He was still sitting there when the lady whisked by with a cheerful wave.

Somehow Creelman's driver managed to turn the carriage upright and get started again. By now the woman was too far ahead for Creelman to catch up with her. Instead he concentrated on crossing out the unnecessary words in the proclamation so he could cable it home at the cheapest rate. His only hope was that the woman would be delayed when she reached the censor's office and had to do the same thing to her dispatch.

The office was in a large stone palace that had been built for the Spanish governor of the Philippines. Creelman dashed through its marble entrance hall, charged up the stairs, and raced down the corridor to the censor's headquarters. The newsman's wife was there ahead of him, her clothes covered with dust, her hair straggling around her face. Just as he had hoped, she was bent over her copy of the proclamation, pencil in hand, trying to condense it to a less expensive length.

Creelman still hadn't finished shortening his own dispatch, but he marched over to the soldier on duty and hurled it on his desk. The man took one look at it and gasped. "You're going to cable the whole thing?" he said incredulously.

Creelman had hoped to hide his decision from his rival, but the soldier refused to heed his gestures for secrecy. "It'll cost money to cable that," he insisted and, still clucking in disbelief, took the dispatch in for the censor's approval.

Once Creelman received permission to send out the proclamation, he still had to travel another two and a half miles from the censor to the cable office. The newsman hired a second carriage outside the palace and started on his way. A branch office of the cable company was much closer, but Creelman had a good reason for deciding the main station would be better.

As he burst into the cable office, the correspondent saw that none of the telegraphs were busy. That meant his rival had not yet sent her story from the branch office. Creelman rushed over to the desk. "I want to hold all the wires," he announced breathlessly. "I'm willing to pay the price."

The words were barely out of his mouth when the wire from the branch office started to click. The operator looked at it helplessly. Creelman already had first call on every wire out of Manila.

Halting the clicking wireless, the operator started to send the correspondent's dispatch. Still nervous about missing a scoop, Creelman decided to cable it at the urgent rate—a staggering nine times more than the regular price.

Creelman groaned inwardly at the thought of the bill he was running up, but he knew he had won the race. Even if his rival used the urgent rate now, Creelman's message would still be the first to arrive in New York.

As Creelman turned to leave the cable office, the woman herself walked in. She knew at once what had happened, but her manner was completely unruffled.

"I suppose you've been cabling a few words," she said lightly.

Creelman was equally nonchalant.

"Oh, just a little message to let them know I'm alive," he replied with a perfectly straight face.

The triumph of the occasion vanished, however, when he turned to leave the office. "That message of yours," the manager whispered, "will cost just seven thousand, six hundred and two dollars and forty-two cents in silver."

"It was my first race with a woman," James Creelman said in his book *On the Great Highway.* "Heaven save me from another!"

Later Creelman served as a magazine and then a newspaper editor, as well as head of New York City's Civil Service Commission for two years. Eventually, however, he returned to his first love—reporting. In 1915, the *New York American* sent him to Berlin to cover the Great War in Europe. But Creelman contracted pleurisy on the voyage over and died in Germany a few days after his arrival.

The runaway boy from Montreal had traveled a long way in his fifty-six years. It was tragic, but fitting, that the road ended while he was on his way to another story.

7

Richard Harding Davis

When Richard Harding Davis embarked on his first assignment as a war correspondent, he was already a successful short-story writer. He was also regarded as one of the most glamorous men in New York.

Dick Davis was born in Philadelphia in 1864. His mother, Rebecca Harding Davis, was a well-known fiction writer, his father an editor on the *Philadelphia Inquirer*. Their oldest son, not surprisingly, decided to follow in his parents' footsteps. The only obstacle to Davis's career as a journalist, however, was school. Dick simply could not master the intricacies of spelling, mathematics baffled him, and history, he always maintained, was something you could look up in a book when you had some use for it.

Despite his complete incompetence as a student, Dick Davis had an honest, straightforward manner that endeared him to the faculty at the private school he attended. He was, in addition, a superb athlete—which endeared him to the students. Davis somehow managed to squeeze through high school and get accepted at Swarthmore College. He did so poorly in his freshman year, however, that he had to return to high school for another year of preparation. After that he entered Lehigh University.

Although he became a star halfback on Lehigh's football team, Davis's bad marks once again caught up with him and he was expelled in his junior year. After another equally disastrous experience at Johns Hopkins University, Richard Harding Davis returned home and, through his father's influence, went to work for the *Philadelphia Record*.

Impeccably dressed and unfailingly polite, the cub reporter cut an odd figure in the rough, tough newspaper world of that era. He was not a particularly hard worker, but he always suspected—and with good reason—that he was fired from his first job primarily because he insisted on wearing kid gloves to work.

Davis soon found another job on the *Philadelphia Press*. Chastened by his failure on the *Record,* he took off his kid gloves and began to take reporting seriously. Before long, he had developed into such an able newspaperman that he was ready to move on to the more challenging world of New York.

Dick Davis came to New York in December, 1889, and went to work for the *Evening Sun.* There he became famous, not for covering fires on the Bowery or robberies in Brooklyn, but for a series of short features he wrote about the adventures of a fictitious New York bachelor-about-town, Mr. Cortland Van Bibber. Van Bibber went to the opera in top hat and satin-lined Inverness cape, strolled along Fifth Avenue with the prettiest debutantes, and quaffed champagne at Delmonico's, Martin's, and other fashionable restaurants of the day.

The name Richard Harding Davis became even better known with the publication of the widely acclaimed short story "Gallegher" in *Scribner's Magazine.* That and the Van

Bibber stories made their author a celebrity, and he was soon enjoying a style of life much like that of his debonair hero.

The twenty-six-year-old reporter at last felt free to indulge his taste for kid gloves and tailor-made suits. He had his own table at Delmonico's, and the other diners—especially the women—craned their necks to catch a glimpse of him. His enemies accused Davis of being conceited and overbearing. At times he was both, but he could also be amazingly thoughtful and kind.

Once he was sent to take a contribution from the *Evening Sun*'s charity fund to a needy family on Thirty-fourth Street. Davis was so moved by the family's plight that he gave them every cent he had in his pockets and was forced to walk all the way back downtown to his office. On another occasion, his sister Nora told him about a new teacher at one of Philadelphia's private schools whose students had snubbed her at church. The next time Davis was home for a visit, he appeared at the church door and escorted the young woman home, leaving her pupils openmouthed with envy and chagrin.

In 1892, Dick Davis moved from the *Evening Sun* to the Harper publishing house. The new job suited him perfectly. He was to spend part of each year as managing editor of *Harper's Weekly*, the other part traveling around the world writing articles for *Harper's Monthly*. For the next few years, Davis saw and did practically everything exciting there was to do in life. Then, in 1896, William Randolph Hearst offered him a chance to savor a new adventure—war.

Hearst wanted Davis to spend a month reporting on the insurrection in Cuba for the *New York Journal*. Davis, always eager for excitement, accepted the assignment, but he soon discovered that war was a far from romantic adventure. Although he was rarely close to the fighting, he saw ruined villages, weeping women, and starving children. Davis wrote several dispatches recounting the tragic plight of the embattled island, but his work for the *Journal* ended abruptly when one of his stories was grossly misinterpreted and given the sensationalist treatment that was Hearst's specialty. Davis resigned indignantly and offered his services to the *Journal's* chief rival, the *World*.

Davis was disappointed not to have seen more military action in Cuba, but he made up for it the following year. When Greece and Turkey went to war over Crete, he was flattered to receive an offer to report the conflict for the prestigious London *Times*.

During the climactic battle of Velestinos, the correspondent spent thirteen hours in a soggy trench. Greek infantrymen fell to his left and right, but the only thing that hit Davis was a shower of mud from a shell that landed less than three feet away. After the battle, Davis had to be carried from the field with sciatica—a painful disease of the nerves in the thighs. Nevertheless, he managed to write a description of Velestinos in the style that was to become his trademark as a war correspondent. Instead of discussing military strategy or the significance of the victory, Dick Davis wrote a simple human-interest story built around a Greek peasant boy who was experiencing his first taste of war.

When the fighting in Greece was over, Davis was happy to return to London. He had many friends in England and, at one dinner party he attended, he noticed that his hostess had decorated the table with red and yellow tulips. Davis smiled. It might soon be considered bad taste, he remarked, to place the colors of Spain on a table where an American was dining.

As the correspondent had anticipated, the United States soon entered Cuba's revolt against Spain. Davis covered the war for both *The Times* of London and the *New York Herald*.

One of his first stories described the bombardment of a Spanish shore battery that he had witnessed from the deck of Admiral William T. Sampson's flagship, the U.S.S. *New York*. When the cease-fire sounded and before the gun smoke had completely cleared away, a *Herald* dispatch boat nosed in beside the big warship. Davis tossed his story down in a weighted envelope, and the converted tugboat chugged off to Key West, Florida, and a telegraph line to New York.

The reporter had scored a scoop, but he complained in a letter to his parents that he had been forced to write the story in fifteen minutes "so it was no good except that we had it exclusively."

Richard Harding Davis's most vivid story from Cuba described the charge of the First Volunteer Cavalry—better known as the Rough Riders—at San Juan Hill. He was particularly impressed by one of the colonels of the regiment, a former assistant secretary of the navy named Theodore Roosevelt. "Roosevelt," he wrote, "mounted high on horseback and charging the rifle pits at a gallop and quite alone, made you feel that you would like to cheer. He wore on his sombrero a blue polka-dot handkerchief . . . which, as he advanced, floated straight behind his head like a guidon."

During another battle near Santiago, Davis was again plagued by sciatica and spent most of the time on the grass writhing in pain. He struggled to his feet, however, when he saw his fellow correspondent, the novelist Stephen Crane, standing in the line of enemy fire. Davis lunged at Crane and knocked him to a safer position on the ground. As he did, Davis's hat went spinning off under the impact of one bullet, and a second shot ripped through the leather case in which he carried his field glasses.

Davis, even in battle the aristocrat from Delmonico's, was totally unperturbed by his narrow escape. Once an excited reporter, with shells whistling overhead and men falling on all sides, grabbed Davis by the arm. "Isn't this awful! Isn't this awful!" he shouted, his voice hoarse with fear.

Dick Davis loosened the man's grip from his sleeve and murmured politely, "Very disturbing. Very disturbing."

The Spanish-American War ended in the summer of 1898, but a little more than a year later there was another war to report. In the fall of 1899, the British and the Boers began fighting in South Africa. This time, Richard Harding Davis arrived to cover the war with his wife at his side. They had been married the previous May. Mrs. Davis, forbidden to go to the front, was left at Cape Town with British poet and novelist Rudyard Kipling and his wife.

Although Dick Davis accompanied the British troops, his sympathies were with the Boers. Their cause, he felt, was much like that of the Cubans or even the Americans themselves during the War for Independence. In the middle of the war, Davis abruptly requested permission from the British to continue his reporting from the Boer side. It was an unheard-of switch, but the British, who resented his critical articles, were grateful to be rid of him. The Boers, aware that such a distinguished member of the press as Richard Harding Davis was a powerful ally, welcomed him and even agreed to let his wife accompany him to the front.

During one battle, Cecil Davis stood beside her husband and watched the Boers retreat before a British column commanded by Lord Roberts. She remained calm despite shrapnel bursting all around her and refused to flee until the British were within five hundred yards of their observation post. Davis vowed that this would be his wife's first and last experience under fire. When he went to Japan in 1904, Mrs. Davis remained at home.

Davis was in the Orient to report on the Russo-Japanese

War over Manchuria. The war marked the beginning of a less free and easy style of war reporting. The Japanese army not only had strict rules of censorship, but it also refused to let correspondents go anywhere without official permission.

Davis, disgusted, spent most of his time writing travel pieces about life in Tokyo. Once he and some other correspondents were taken to Manchuria, but the closest they got to the war was a hillside where, with the help of field glasses, they could dimly make out the smoke of the guns in the distance. Davis said it was the only battle he had ever seen "that did not require you to calmly smoke a pipe in order to conceal the fact that you were scared."

The final battle in the war between Russia and Japan appeared to be shaping up at Liaoyang. When Davis requested permission to go there, he was told by a Japanese officer that the Russians had retreated without resistance and the Japanese had already taken the town. Several other newsmen refused to believe the story and sneaked off to Liaoyang. Davis did not. Assuming the war was over, he made his way to the Manchurian coast to wire his editor that he was coming home.

As soon as Davis walked into the cable office, the operator offered his congratulations. Davis, he said, was the first correspondent to arrive with the story of the battle.

Davis shook his head. "There was no battle," he said. "The Japanese told me themselves they entered Liaoyang without firing a shot."

The operator broke the news as gently as possible. "They have been fighting for six days," he said quietly.

Dick Davis had missed Japan's victory in the greatest battle since the defeat of the French at Sedan in the Franco-Prussian War.

Although Davis himself was sorely disappointed with his

reporting of the Russo-Japanese War, his reputation at home remained untarnished. At forty he still possessed the lean, square-jawed good looks that had inspired illustrator Charles Dana Gibson to use him as the model for the young man who paid court to the famous swan-necked Gibson girls of the early 1900s.

Moreover, he was rapidly growing rich. He had several plays produced on Broadway, a single short story brought him a thousand dollars, and for special news articles his rate was as high as twenty-five cents a word. "Think of getting fifty cents for writing 'for instance,'" he wrote to one of his friends.

Richard Harding Davis's personal life ran less smoothly, though. His father, and then his mother—to whom he was especially close—died. His wife, Cecil, divorced him. Davis tried to lose himself in writing still more short stories, novels, and plays. Eventually his gloom disappeared and in 1912 he remarried. His new wife was a beautiful, vivacious actress whom he worshiped until his death.

In the spring of 1914, after several misunderstandings with Mexico, President Woodrow Wilson sent the American fleet steaming southward and ordered several brigades of the U.S. Army to stand by in Texas. It looked as if the two countries would go to war. If they did, Richard Harding Davis wanted to be on hand to write about it.

As it turned out, the dispute with Mexico was settled without a fight. Davis caused a sensation, however, when he arrived in the tense and battered city of Veracruz soon after it had been shelled by American warships. That night, Davis ate his dinner at the café in front of the Hotel Diligencia. He dined in evening clothes, a bottle of vintage champagne resting in a cooler at his elbow. Half the town came out to gape at the strange *gringo*.

After his brief visit to Mexico, Davis settled down at his country house near Mount Kisco, New York. The tranquillity of his life at Crossroads Farm was interrupted, however, when, in the summer of 1914, Europe went to war. It would be Richard Harding Davis's sixth war—and his last. But it was also the war in which he would do his finest reporting.

Davis was in Brussels when the Germans marched into the city. "For three days and three nights," he wrote, "the column of gray with hundreds of thousands of bayonets and hundreds of thousands of lances, with gray transport wagons, gray ammunition carts, gray ambulances, gray cannon, like a river of steel, cut Brussel in two."

The Germans had little use for American war correspondents. They relented enough to give Davis a pass, but his orders were to stay within the vicinity of Brussels. Davis promptly disobeyed them and set off in search of a story.

As he swaggered along the road out of Brussels, he looked for all the world like a British officer in civilian clothes. He was wearing an English-made suit and, to make matters worse, the picture on his passport showed him wearing a military tunic much like one that was worn by British regiments; he was also sporting an impressive collection of campaign ribbons on his chest.

Davis had not gone far when he found himself in the midst of a large force of Germans. One of their officers examined his papers and, after forcing him to march for five hours with the advancing troops, finally sent him off in a car with several other officers. One of them—a sinister-looking man whom Davis immediately dubbed "Rupert" after the villain in a book he had read—accused him of being a British spy. The evidence, the German insisted, was perfectly clear. His passport picture showed him wearing a British uniform.

Davis explained that he had ordered the outfit several years before, copying it from one that was worn by the British West African Field Force in the Boer War. Since then, several other regiments had adopted the style.

Rupert looked at him with a sneer. "Do you expect me to believe that?" he snarled.

Davis grinned. "Listen," he said, "if you could invent an explanation for that uniform as quickly as I told you that one, standing in a road with eight officers trying to shoot you, you would be the greatest general in Germany."

The other officers laughed at Davis's quick rejoinder, but Rupert was not to be put off so easily. "If you are not a British officer," he demanded, pointing to the passport photo, "why are you wearing those campaign ribbons on your chest?"

Davis explained that they were correspondents' ribbons, but Rupert dismissed the explanation with another sneer and ordered him put under armed guard.

Davis thought the next step was sure to be the firing squad, but he had an idea that might save him. If the Germans would let him go, he promised to return to Brussels. They could affix a note to his pass ordering him to be shot if he was found off the main road or if he failed to complete the fifty-mile trip within the next two days.

To Davis's amazement, the German accepted his terms. His friend Rupert called him in at midnight and told him he could leave in three hours. The prospect was not much better than the firing squad. Anyone wandering near an army camp in the dark stood a good chance of being shot on sight.

Richard Harding Davis started down the main road to Brussels at three o'clock that morning. He spoke no German, so every time he came to a sentry he lit a match and held it next to the red correspondent's seal on his pass. Miraculously the soldiers held their fire. In the morning he was lucky enough to meet a German general who, without even asking to see his credentials, offered him a ride to Brussels in his staff car.

Davis arrived at the American legation unshaven and footsore, with a bright red sunburn on his handsome face. But he was so grateful to be alive that he didn't complain about not being his usual dapper self.

Soon after that, Davis left Brussels and took a train for Holland. On the morning of his departure, the German commander in chief ordered the city of Louvain destroyed because a group of Belgian civilians had fired on his soldiers. Davis's train passed right through Louvain and he was able to watch the destruction of the historic city from the window of his railroad car.

He saw the Germans systematically setting fire to the houses and watched while men were marched off to a firing squad, their wives and children following them in tears. When at last the train moved on, Davis had been without food for twenty-six hours, but he had a news story that was one of the most dramatic of the entire war.

Davis next decided to go to Paris. The French refused to give him a correspondent's pass, so he made up his own papers, decorating them with the impressive red seals he had stolen from the government's official war bulletins.

With two other correspondents, Davis hired a taxi to drive to Soissons, where they watched the Allied fight to recapture the city from the Germans. The next day the other reporters decided to continue to cover Soissons, but Davis preferred Reims. The only thing he knew about the city was that it had a famous cathedral, but his instinct told him that Reims was the place to be.

As he approached the city, the magnificent cathedral towered over the other buildings and dominated the landscape. Davis found Reims a mass of smoke and crumbled masonry. The Germans had been forced to retreat and had retaliated by shelling the city. The cathedral's statues were smashed, its rich, stained-glass windows splintered, and pieces of stone from its Gothic spires littered the great square in which it stood. Despite the damage, one of the priests had set up a shelter in the cathedral for the wounded soldiers the Germans had left behind.

Davis spent twenty-four hours under bombardment in Reims. He visited the city again a few days later. By then the roof of the cathedral had caught fire from the shells. The archbishop of Reims had to stand on the steps of the burning building and turn back an angry mob who wanted to take vengeance on the wounded German soldiers for the destruction of the city.

Davis rushed back to Paris with his story, but before he could file it the French discovered that his correspondent's pass was a forgery and sent him off to jail. Ironically, when he was released and finally reached the censor's office the next day, the Frenchman took one look at the dispatch and stopped all the wires. "I insist this go at once," he cried. "It should have been sent twenty-four hours ago."

After the tragic things he had seen at Louvain and Reims, Richard Harding Davis returned to America and became a crusader for his own country's entry into the World War. He made one final trip to Europe, but came home sick and exhausted. One night, as he was making a phone call from Crossroads Farm to a friend in New York, Davis slumped over on his desk and died of a heart attack.

Once again Richard Harding Davis made headlines. There was scarcely a newspaper in the country that did not run his obituary on the front page. But it was William Randolph Hearst's *New York Journal*—the paper Davis had refused to work for after his first trip to Cuba—that best summed up his life:

"He gave pleasure to many.

"He worked hard for his success and deserved it.

"He was a courageous man."

8

Floyd Gibbons

One afternoon in 1912 a hulking six-footer with a dirty, rumpled suit and two days' growth of beard sauntered into the offices of the *Chicago Tribune*. The man, who looked more like a bum than anything else, insisted that he was an experienced reporter desperately in need of a job. He got one, but only because the head of the copy desk remembered having worked with him on a paper in Minneapolis and put in a good word with the city editor. No longer down and out, Floyd Gibbons cheerfully requested an advance on his first week's salary so he could treat himself to a shave, a haircut, and a new suit of clothes.

Floyd Gibbons was twenty-six years old when he went to work for the *Chicago Tribune*. He had attended Georgetown University in his native Washington, D.C., but left without graduating. Determined to become a reporter, he struck out for the Midwest in search of a job. After working for two papers in Minneapolis and one in Milwaukee, he finally found his way to Chicago and the offices of the *Tribune*.

The *Tribune* was a lively place to work in those days. The self-proclaimed "World's Greatest Newspaper" had an irascible city editor who would fly into a rage at any reporter who failed to come up with a story worthy of the slogan. Gibbons spent two years covering riots and robberies in brawling, sprawling Chicago before he decided that life in a hectic city at the mercy of an explosive editor was much too tame.

In 1914 the Mexican bandit and revolutionary, Pancho Villa, began terrorizing his own country and threatening to raid American towns along the Rio Grande as well. No one knew what Villa was up to, and there seemed no way to find out. The guerrilla leader had sent out word from his mountain headquarters that any *gringos* found in Mexico would be shot on sight.

It was the right sort of challenge and Floyd Gibbons rushed toward the border. He located Villa's hideout and walked alone into the hills. Not only was he not shot, but he came out with an exclusive interview with the rebel leader himself. Not content with that feat, Gibbons tried another. Fitting out a railroad boxcar, he attached it to a train that the revolutionists had captured and rode into the thick of three of Pancho Villa's most important battles. Floyd Gibbons arrived back in Chicago with the only eyewitness account of Villa's war in Mexico.

Gibbons's experiences in Mexico were only a warm-up for more hazardous jobs. In February, 1917, the *Chicago Tribune* sent him to London to report on England's part in the World War. The Germans had repeatedy demonstrated their hostility toward the United States, and Gibbons realized that it was only a matter of time before a particularly bad incident would provoke Congress into declaring war.

On January 31, 1917, the Imperial German Government announced that after February 1 its submarines would sink without warning any ship that ventured into a certain area of the North Atlantic. Gibbons realized at once that the ultimatum meant trouble. There were several liners on which he could book passage. One of them would be carrying the German ambassador to the United States back to his homeland. That one was sure to be safe, thought Gibbons. He bypassed it and selected instead the eighteen-thousand-ton Cunard liner, *Laconia*.

Along with his baggage, he carried his own life preserver, a flashlight, a container of fresh water, and a flask of brandy. If, as he expected, the *Laconia* was torpedoed, Floyd Gibbons was prepared for it.

On February 25 the ship was about two hundred miles off the coast of Ireland, just inside the German danger zone. Gibbons, who was in the *Laconia*'s smoking room around 10:30 P.M., idly asked another passenger what he thought the ship's chances were of being torpedoed.

"I should say about four thousand to one," the man replied.

A few minutes later there was a crunching sound from somewhere amidships and the giant liner gave a sudden lurch. In another minute, the *Laconia*'s whistle began to bellow ominously through the darkness. Five short blasts—the signal to abandon ship. There was surprisingly little panic. Gibbons made his way to the lifeboats with the rest of the passengers. The boats were lowered and the frightened survivors found themselves huddled together in the small craft bobbing about in the giant swells.

"It was about a half hour after we heard the report of the first torpedo that we heard another dull thud," Gibbons reported later. "The German submarine had dispatched another torpedo. This time it penetrated the vitals of the ship, directly into the engine room.

"We watched silently during the next minutes as the *La-*

conia's tiers of lights dimmed slowly from white to yellow, then to red. And then nothing was left, nothing but the shroud of the night which hung over us like a pall."

The passengers in the lifeboat started to row in a direction they hoped was shoreward. "We steadied the boat's head into the wind," the reporter continued, "and a black hulk moved toward us and stopped about ten feet away. It was the 'sub.' "

A man's head appeared in the conning tower and a voice with a heavy German accent inquired, "What ship was that?"

Someone told him it was the *Laconia*. The officer wanted to know its size, how many passengers it carried, and whether its captain was among the survivors in the lifeboat. Then the U-boat slithered off into the night.

"Hours passed," Gibbon reported. "We bailed constantly. Most of us were wet to the knees and shivering from the weakening effects of the icy water. Our hands were blistered from pulling at the oars. Our stomachs ached from vain retching. We had only sea biscuit to eat."

After six hours in the open boat in the freezing North Atlantic, someone at last sighted a light. Gibbons called it "a blessed beacon that beamed like the Christmas star to the wise men."

The light grew gradually larger and, after what seemed like ages, a British minesweeper appeared through the blackness and took the twenty-three half-frozen survivors aboard. The boat had already picked up most of the other 73 passengers and 216 crew members, but 13 people were never found.

Once on shore, Floyd Gibbons made a hurried dash to the cable office and wired a four-thousand-word description of the *Laconia*'s sinking back to the *Chicago Tribune*. The paper syndicated the story and distributed it to hundreds of newspapers all over the United States. Although the *Laconia* was a British liner, Americans were horrified that the Germans would torpedo a passenger ship with women and children aboard. The incident was an important factor in America's decision to enter the war less than six weeks later.

When the commander of the American Expeditionary Forces, Major General John J. Pershing, debarked from the Cunard liner *Baltic,* Floyd Gibbons was among the reporters on the Liverpool pier. British censors, keeping a close watch on the press, forbade reporters to mention Pershing's port of arrival in their dispatches. The irrepressible Gibbons wrote out a cable to the *Chicago Tribune* and gleefully watched it pass the unsuspecting censor's eye. It said: "Pershing landed at British port today and was greeted by lord mayor of Liverpool."

Gibbons accompanied Pershing's army across the channel to France, but it was some time before American correspondents were allowed anywhere near the front. Whiling away the dull days in Paris, Gibbons and his fellow reporters spent most of their time playing cards and arguing with their perennial enemies, the military censors. Just to break the monotony, the newsmen decided to attend a Fourth of July ceremony at which General Pershing was to lay a wreath on Lafayette's tomb in a small cemetery just outside Paris.

One of the general's aides, Major Charles E. Stanton, made a rousing speech at the ceremony, concluding with the stirring words, "Lafayette, we are here!" Pershing, a man of few words, followed him, murmuring only that Major Stanton had echoed the sentiments of Americans everywhere.

What followed may have been an honest mistake. More likely it was a newsman's desire to enliven an otherwise routine dispatch, but Floyd Gibbons cabled home an account in which Stanton's "Lafayette, we are here!" was attributed to General Pershing. It was a perfect story for the Fourth of July; unfortunately, the confusion has remained ever since.

The American correspondents hung around Paris for weeks waiting for the army's permission to go to the front. When the order finally came through late in October, Floyd Gibbon had disappeared. His friends were baffled. "Poor Gib," one of them said. "He isn't here to move up with us."

"It's the first scoop I ever knew him to miss," another muttered, shaking his head.

The correspondents headed out of Paris. Approaching the Western Front, they passed an American artillery detachment. A familiar figure stood next to one of the caissons and an unmistakable face peered out from under a doughboy's cap. "Hey," yelled one of the correspondents, "isn't that Gibbons?"

The *Tribune* correspondent, certain that this particular artillery division would be one of the first to go into action, had arranged to join it as a volunteer private. Gibbons had already seen the first shot fired by an American gun crew. He had commandeered the shell case as a souvenir and was persuaded to give it up only when one of the officers informed him that it had been promised to President Woodrow Wilson.

Enraged at Gibbons's sneaky tactics, the other correspondents turned him in to the military censors. He was clapped into jail for forty-eight hours and—what bothered him most —was not allowed to file his story until all the others were finished.

Floyd Gibbons always maintained that he did his best

reporting when he was personally involved in the events he wrote about. Nervy and fast-talking, he rarely had difficulty arranging to be in the midst of things.

In the spring of 1918, the Germans were making a last desperate attempt to conquer Paris. Most of the fighting centered around Château-Thierry and a large forest called Belleau Wood. To get to the front, Gibbons engaged a sleek car and driver. It gave him an aura of importance that helped him talk his way past dozens of official barriers.

Arriving in Château-Thierry, he pulled up in front of American headquarters and requested permission to continue on to Belleau Wood. The officer he talked to shrugged. "Go wherever you like," he said. "Go as far as you like, but I want to tell you it's darn hot up there."

Gibbons turned to his military escort, Lieutenant Oscar Hartzell. "Let's go," he snapped.

An hour later, the two men crouched in the woods watching a nearby village shrouded in smoke and flames from a German bombardment. Two hundred yards away, another clump of trees concealed a company of enemy troops. Gibbons and Hartzell found a trench occupied by an American machine gun crew and crawled into it to await the battalion commander's order to advance.

When the order arrived a few hours later, it was delivered by a young lieutenant. The man stared at Floyd Gibbons's green armband with the red correspondent's C in the center. "What are you doing here?" he demanded.

"Looking for the big story," Gibbons replied.

"If I were you I'd be about forty miles south of this place," the lieutenant growled, "but if you want to see the fun, stick around. We're going forward in five minutes."

Gibbons watched his trench mates preparing to go over

the top. "There is no bugle call, no sword waving, no dramatic enunciation of catchy commands, no theatricalism—it's just plain get up and go over," he wrote. "And it is done just the same as one would walk across a peaceful wheat field in Iowa."

But Belleau Wood was no peaceful wheat field. The American front line had barely left the shelter of the trees when enemy machine gun fire ripped across the clearing between the two armies. Falling on their stomachs to avoid the barrage, the troops alternately ran and crawled until they reached the German-held position in the opposite wood.

Gibbons and his escort, Lieutenant Hartzell, attached themselves to the battalion commander, Major John Berry, who was going forward with his men. Some of the Germans had been wiped out, but there were still several machine gun nests in the woods to the left and enemy snipers were hiding in the trees. Gibbons was the only unarmed man in Berry's party. He said afterward that he carried a "loaded" notebook.

The men managed to get past their own shelter of trees and out into the open field before the clatter of machine guns rattled across the landscape. Major Berry barked an order for everyone to get down.

Gibbons was sprawled flat on the ground when he heard a shout in front of him. The major had been hit. He struggled to his feet, obviously in great pain, and motioned to his companions. "We've got to get out of here," he cried. "They'll start shelling this field in a few minutes."

Gibbons started crawling toward the wounded major. His plan was to help him to the shelter of some woods along the far edge of the field. Before he could get to Berry he felt a sudden pain. The lighted end of a cigarette seemed to have touched his upper arm. He glanced down at the sleeve of his uniform and saw nothing. Then he felt the burning sensation again, this time in his left shoulder.

Gibbons, not realizing he had been hit, continued crawling toward Major Berry.

Suddenly he felt a crash. It sounded to Gibbons "as if some one had dropped a glass bottle into a porcelain bathtub." The world tipped at a crazy angle and everything turned white.

At first Gibbons thought he was dead. He realized he was not when he caught a glimpse of Major Berry scurrying unaided into the woods. He later learned that the wounded officer had directed his men to wipe out the German machine gun nest that had attacked them. Berry was subsequently awarded the Distinguished Service Cross for his valor.

Meanwhile, Gibbons and Lieutenant Hartzell were still pinned down in the open field. Gibbons called to Hartzell and told him he was hit, but when the lieutenant offered to crawl over and help him Gibbons advised against it. After a hurried conference, the two men decided to play dead and then crawl from the field at nightfall.

"It's six o'clock now," Hartzell said, "and it won't be dark till nine; this is June. Do you think you can stick it out?"

There wasn't much choice. Gibons lay there unaware that his left eye had been torn from its socket. He tried not to think about the wounds in his arm and shoulder, but it was harder to ignore the machine gun bullets that continued to rip across the field only inches above his head. Gibbons knew that each German machine gun was capable of firing three hundred shots a minute. It was not a consoling thought.

The hours between six and nine dragged slowly, but daylight at last faded away and Lieutenant Hartzell called over to Gibbons to tell him they could be on their way. Leaning heavily on the lieutenant's arm, Gibbons staggered across the field and into the safety of the woods. The two men walked for almost a mile before Hartzell found a medical unit. The doctors took one look at the battered correspondent and ordered him removed to a much larger military hospital on the outskirts of Paris.

Floyd Gibbons awoke at eleven o'clock the next morning minus his left eye, his left arm in a sling, but in surprisingly good spirits after his trip "over the top."

One of the first faces the newspaperman saw when he was well enough to get out of bed was the lieutenant who had warned him before the advance that he'd be better off forty miles away. The lieutenant took one look at Gibbons's bandages and sighed, "I told you so."

Gibbons was awarded the Croix de Guerre for his heroism under fire; he was also elected to the French Legion of Honor. But a more constant reminder of his nightmare in Belleau Wood was the white linen patch that covered his missing left eye. He wore it as jauntily as most men wear a flower in their buttonhole.

During the next two decades, the world was troubled by a series of small wars that had their climax in World War II. Floyd Gibbons covered almost all of them. When he appeared in Shanghai in 1932 to report on the conflict between China and Japan, another correspondent remarked, "Now the war is official. Gibbons is here."

In 1935, the Italian dictator, Benito Mussolini, provoked a dispute with the African nation of Ethiopia. Mussolini was using the disagreement to provide an excuse to march into Ethiopia and annex the country to the adjacent Italian colony of Eritrea.

At the outset of the trouble, Floyd Gibbons and another reporter named Webb Miller were the only American correspondents allowed on the scene. Mussolini was so impressed with Gibbons, in fact, that he sent a special army plane to take him to Eritrea from Rome.

An invasion of Ethiopia appeared imminent. While Miller and Gibbons waited for it to begin, their Italian hosts took them on an inspection tour of the military bases along the frontier. Preparations for D day were so well under way that the two correspondents began writing their news stories at once. They were not allowed to send them, however, until war was officially declared at 5:00 A.M. on October 3.

The Italians graciously provided Gibbons and Miller with a protected observation post on a mountainside overlooking the invasion site. They had a ledge of sandbags on which to rest their typewriters, a telegraph operator was on hand to send out bulletins, and not far away a motorcycle messenger waited to rush longer dispatches to a nearby radio station.

The newsmen sent several bulletins as soon as the invasion began. Their longer stories, however, already half-written, had been left at their quarters in Eritrea's capital. The reporters were stunned when, at 9:30 A.M., the Italian motorcyclist suddenly announced that they would have to have the stories ready to go within fifteen minutes.

The two correspondents had been up since two that morning. The temperature on the mountainside had been climbing steadily all morning. At that point it was 118 degrees in the shade. Undaunted, Floyd Gibbons and Webb Miller sat down to cram as much news as possible into fifteen minutes' worth of furious typing.

Somehow they both made it and the stories went off to the radio office. Gibbons was disappointed that Miller's got to New York a few minutes ahead of his, but he was cheered by the fact that both stories arrived hours ahead of any other news of the invasion.

Gibbons was forty-nine years old. Except for the wounds he received at Belleau Wood, he had aways been in the best of health, but now, for the first time in his career, the newsman found himself too exhausted to follow the campaign any further. Ethiopia's severe heat and high altitudes were putting a tremendous strain on his heart.

A year later, Gibbons was well enough to cover the Civil War in Spain, but this time he returned home even faster than he had from Ethiopia. It was not exhaustion that was troubling him, but disgust. The war in Spain was a vicious, heartbreaking struggle. Gibbons came home in less than a month. "It is the bloodiest, costliest war, in men and money, that I have ever seen," he said. "It is horrifying to see how inhuman . . . men can be to each other."

In between his tours of duty as a war correspondent, Floyd Gibbons earned a comfortable living as a radio commentator and newspaper columnist. He continued his work after his return from Spain. Then, in 1939, after all the bullets he had dodged and all the risks he had taken, Floyd Gibbons died quietly of a heart ailment at his farm in Saylorsburg, Pennsylvania.

9

Ernie Pyle

Ernie Pyle was the most unlikely man in the world to have become a war correspondent. He considered warfare senseless and frankly admitted that combat scared him to death. Yet the shy, gnomelike reporter not only wrote about, but shared, the dangers of America's fighting men in the front lines of some of the bloodiest battles of World War II.

Born on August 3, 1900, and officially christened Ernest Taylor Pyle, the future correspondent grew up on his father's farm near Dana, Indiana. A shallow creek meandered through a pasture about a half mile down the road from Will Pyle's property, and on summer days Ernie would slip off his overalls and take a dip in the cool water. It was a good place for fishing, too. Sometimes he didn't even need a hook. Ernie always claimed that the biggest fish he ever caught swam inside his underwear one day. Thinking quickly, he leaped out of the water, removed his trapped quarry, took it home, and ate it for dinner.

One of the most vivid recollections of Ernie Pyle's boyhood was the time he and his best friend, Thad Hooker, went out on their first dates. Thad made all the arrangements. Ernie, a skinny fourteen-year-old redhead, was so nervous at the prospect that he "worried about it all week and would have backed out, but my mother made me go."

It took him almost all afternoon to get dressed, but at last, feeling most uncomfortable in his hard collar and new brown suit, he climbed into the Hookers' surrey and he and Thad went forth to meet their fate. The date consisted of going to church services and then returning to one of the girls' houses for a game of Authors. "After that," as Ernie described it some years later, "the whole thing sort of bogged down. We couldn't think of anything to say, and we wanted to go home but didn't know how to get started."

The boys were finally rescued when their hostess's mother appeared at the parlor door and motioned her daughter to step outside. A few minutes later the girl reappeared, giggling and holding up an alarm clock. Thad and Ernie instantly leaped to their feet and rushed to the door. "We said something about not knowing it was so late," Ernie said, "and rushed out."

Ernie Pyle was a junior in high school when the United States went to war against Germany in 1917. His friend Thad Hooker joined the army right away, but Will and Marie Pyle insisted that their son stay home and finish high school first. Ernie was heartsick. At graduation there was an empty flag-draped chair on the stage for Thad and, said his best friend, "I could hardly bear to go to commencement. I was so ashamed that I wasn't in the army too."

Not long after he received his diploma, Ernie enlisted in the Naval Reserve, but when the armistice was signed in November, his unit was disbanded and the would-be sailor found himself back on the farm. He had no particular plans for the future. The only thing he knew for certain was that he did not want to be a farmer. He had had enough of feeding hogs and plowing fields and struggling out of a sound sleep at four o'clock in the morning.

Ernie's marks in school had been good, and Will and Marie Pyle agreed to let him go on to the state university at Bloomington. He arrived on the campus in the fall of 1919, an awkward country boy in ill-fitting clothes. Ernie had always been fascinated by automobiles, and the first thing that impressed him about college life was the number of cars he saw on the streets of Bloomington. "There is a lot of big fine machines down here," he wrote in one of his first letters home.

Someone told the freshman that journalism was an easy major, so he signed up for it at the beginning of his sophomore year. Ernie's real love, however, was travel. He was itching to see something beyond the flat midwestern farmland he had been looking at all his life.

His first chance came when Indiana University's baseball team was invited to Japan in 1922. Borrowing two hundred dollars and finagling himself a job on the steamship, Ernie not only accompanied the team but reported on the trip for the campus newspaper, the *Student*. He mailed in his first story, signed with his first by-line, soon after the boat sailed. The biggest news was that almost all the Indiana men, including himself, were seasick.

Only a few minutes before he was scheduled to graduate, Ernie heard of an opening for a reporter on the La Porte, Indiana, *Herald*. The job paid twenty-five dollars a week and, despite his parents' complaints about his quitting school, Ernie decided to take it. When he arrived in La Porte, the boss took one look at his new employee and almost changed his mind. "I thought we had picked a lemon," he confessed later. "This young man, bashful and unimpressive, didn't look like a newspaperman to us."

The editor was desperate, however, so he put the "lemon" to work covering city hall, the courthouse, and the police and fire stations. To his amazement, everybody in town seemed to like Ernie, and the cub reporter's stories were soon making the front pages. Ernie did so well that a few months later he was able to graduate to a better-paying job on the *Daily News* in Washington, D.C.

Living in the big city did nothing to improve the Indiana farm boy's appearance. He often showed up at his desk wearing a plaid lumberjack's shirt, with a white wool stocking cap perched on his head. Once Roy Howard, president of the vast Scripps-Howard newspaper chain to which the *News* belonged, walked into the Washington office and spied the strangely attired reporter. "What's *that*?" he growled.

As a tribute to his talent rather than his tailoring, Ernie was eventually made managing editor of the *News*. Instead of being excited about the promotion, he was plunged in gloom. Ernie's two pet hates were routine and responsibility; both of them came with the managing editor's job. Moreover, he had developed an almost fanatic interest in airplanes and in 1928 had launched what was probably the first daily aviation column in the country. Now he would have to give it up.

Ernie's flier friends were as disappointed as he was at the news of his promotion. A group of them invited him out to the Washington airport one day for a touching farewell ceremony. The world-famous pilot, Amelia Earhart, made a brief speech and presented Ernie with a watch that he wore for the rest of his life.

Somehow Pyle survived in the managing editor's job for almost two years. Then, in the winter of 1934, he developed a bad case of the flu and couldn't seem to recuperate. "Go someplace warm, like Arizona," his doctor advised.

Ernie and his wife Jerry, a pretty government secretary whom he had married in 1925, set out in their brand-new Ford coupé. After driving through the entire Southwest and encountering nothing but drizzle and clouds, they finally took a freighter from Los Angeles back through the Panama Canal and home.

But the trip had a happy ending. It gave Ernie enough material for a series of columns, which he promptly sold to the *Daily News*. On the strength of these, he persuaded his boss to find a new managing editor and give him a job as a roving reporter.

On the day before his thirty-fifth birthday, Ernie and Jerry once again set out in their Ford. Ernie's assignment was to drive wherever he wanted, write about whatever he pleased. He was to turn out six columns a week and mail them back to Washington for distribution to the twenty-four Scripps-Howard newspapers throughout the country.

The columns covered every imaginable subject. In New Jersey, Ernie wrote about the Lindbergh kidnap trial. In Washington he interviewed Secretary of State Cordell Hull and attended an opening session of the Supreme Court. Once he visited an old friend who was in a Virginia penitentiary, and another time he wrote a nostalgic description of a small boy and his dog. "The little boy had no brothers or sisters to play with. His dog was his constant companion. And in all that vast prairie there was no one who understood the child's mind better than did the dog Shep. . . . When a little boy whose feelings were hurt would go out into the yard and lie down and cry, the dog would go and lie beside him and lick his face in the most complete and understanding sympathy."

Ernie and Jerry were in Portland, Oregon, when war broke out in Europe in the fall of 1939. Although many newspapermen eagerly volunteered to cover the fighting, Ernie was perfectly content to continue his roving assignments. It was around this time that he visited Panama, the site of a large U.S. military base. Ernie hoped he could overlook it in his columns. "If there is one thing in this world I hate and detest," he said at the time, "it is writing about the army."

As a teen-ager during World War I, Ernie Pyle had been eager to serve his country. By the time America found itself fighting a second world war, however, he was a thin, nervous man of forty-one. War was no longer an adventure or even a crusade. "When you figure how many boys are going to get killed," he said once, "what's the use of it anyway?"

Ernie had gone over to England in 1940 and written some excellent pieces about the German air raids on London. Now, when a detachment of American troops was sent to Great Britain, he decided to return. There were two reasons for his decision. The first was his constant search for material for his columns. The second was a need to take his mind off his personal problems. His wife Jerry had suffered a mental breakdown and would be in and out of hospitals until her death in 1945.

Originally, the columnist had no intention of becoming a front-line correspondent, but when the men he had become friendly with in England moved out to take part in the invasion of North Africa he suddenly decided that it was his duty to go along.

More than seventy war correspondents covered the fighting in North Africa, but all of them concentrated on battle strategy and the progress of the campaign itself. Only Ernie Pyle chose to write a different kind of story. Clad in overalls, a long peaked cap, and a soldier's mackinaw, lugging his own bedroll and driving his own jeep, Ernie would travel from one post to another, chatting with the men, sharing their rations, listening to their gripes. He never tried to get a story. He just made friends and somehow the stories came. The "little guy," the soldiers called him. They appreciated the way he explained their loneliness and misery to the folks back home.

"The discomfort is perpetual," he wrote once. "You're always cold and almost always dirty. Outside of food and cigarettes you have absolutely none of the little things that made life normal back home. You don't have chairs, lights, floors, or tables. You don't have any place to set anything, or any store to buy things from. There are no newspapers, milk, beds, sheets, radiators, beer, ice cream, or hot water. You just sort of exist, either standing up working or lying down asleep. There is no pleasant in-between. The velvet is all gone from living. . . ."

Once Ernie spent a week with an army battalion in the rocky hills outside of Bizerte, in North Africa. It was here that he fell in love with the United States Infantry.

"I love the infantry," he wrote, "because they are the underdogs. They are the mud-rain-frost-and-wind boys. They have no comforts, and they even learn to live without the necessities. And in the end they are the guys that wars can't be won without."

Pyle abandoned the army to cover the Allied invasion of Sicily from the deck of the navy flagship *Biscayne*. After three days at sea he was glad to get back to his regular routine—"the old soldier's way of sleeping on the ground and not washing before breakfast and fighting off fleas."

Soon after the Sicilian campaign ended in the summer of 1943, Ernie Pyle, looking even frailer than his 110 pounds, his red hair now turned to white, came home for a rest. He was a national celebrity. A Hollywood producer wanted to talk to him about a movie based on one of the books that had been compiled from his columns; radio networks begged him to appear on the air; autograph hunters waited in the lobby of his Washington hotel.

Eventually, Ernie managed to extricate himself from the furore and retreat to the small house in Albuquerque, New Mexico, that he and Jerry had built just before he went off to war. He described his return to the place in a newspaper column:

"Our little house is still a gem. Now it has some Algerian rugs on the floor, Moroccan hassocks before the fireplace, Congo ivory on the mantel. We can still see eighty miles from our front window, and the sunsets are still spellbinding. Quail still peck in our front yard. Roaming neighborhood dogs come and visit us. So do children. The postman always has something pleasant to say. We have two cups of hot tea very early in the morning, and we are sitting here drinking it when the first dawn comes over the Sandias. The sun soon warms the desert, and the day grows lazy. . . ."

In October Ernie was off again. This time his destination was Italy, where Nazi troops were still fighting a fierce rear-guard action against the Allied invasion forces. Back in the mud with his foot soldiers, Ernie often complained that he had "lost the touch" and was writing the "same old stuff." The "stuff" he grumbled about included one of his most memorable columns, the story of an army captain who was killed in the mountains near San Pietro in December, 1943.

"In this war," he wrote, "I have known a lot of officers who were loved and respected by the soldiers under them. But never have I crossed the trail of any man as beloved as Captain Henry T. Waskow of Belton, Texas."

Pyle told how, after the captain's body had been brought down from the mountains, one by one his men stepped forward. "Not so much to look, I think, as to say something in finality to him, and to themselves. I stood close by and I could hear."

The first few soldiers muttered despairing curses. Then another man said simply, "I'm sorry, old man," and still another, "I sure am sorry, sir."

"Then the first man squatted down, and he reached down and took the dead hand, and he sat there for five full minutes, holding the dead hand in his own, and looked intently into the dead face and he never uttered a sound all the time he sat there.

"And then finally he put the hand down, and then reached up and gently straightened the points of the captain's shirt collar, and then he sort of rearranged the tattered edges of his uniform around the wound. And then he got up and walked away down the road in the moonlight, all alone."

In the spring of 1944 Ernie Pyle flew to London, where he received the news that he had been awarded a Pulitzer Prize for "distinguished correspondence." Knowing that his editor, Lee Miller, was going to submit the columns to the prize jury, Ernie had already bet Miller a hundred dollars that he wouldn't win. When a reporter from the Associated Press called Pyle and told him the good news, he was so stunned that all he could say was, "Now I lose a hundred dollars."

A few weeks later, Ernie Pyle received a call in his room at the Dorchester Hotel. The army officer on the other end of the line was brief. Pyle was to assemble with full field kit at a secret checkpoint. "Be there at ten-thirty hours," the voice barked.

It was then nine o'clock, but Ernie, who had been expecting the call for days, had no trouble collecting his equipment. In a matter of minutes, he was on his way.

It was no secret that the long-planned Allied invasion of

France was going to take place any day. Whispered rumors had been making the rounds of London pubs for weeks. The invasion, code-named operation "Overlord," promised to be the war story of the century, and some 450 American newspapermen had arrived in England hoping to get a firsthand look at the battle. It was decided that only twenty-eight of the men would be allowed to go in with the first assault. One of them was Ernie Pyle.

As the correspondents stood waiting for the jeeps that would take them to their embarkation point, a friend of Ernie's cheerfully whipped out his pencil and notebook and in mock seriousness said to his fellow reporter, "Tell me, Mr. Pyle, how does it feel to be an assault correspondent?"

Ernie wasted no words. "It feels pretty awful," he said.

The invasion site was the coast of Normandy, near the Cotentin Peninsula. After the bitter battle of Omaha Beach, Pyle walked for a mile and a half along the Normandy coast. The beach was littered with dead bodies, sunken landing craft, useless equipment. A "shoreline museum of carnage," Pyle called it.

In Normandy, he also picked up a funny story about an exhausted private who rolled up in his blanket in a field one night and woke up the next morning to find himself lying with a dead German on his right and an unexploded hand grenade on his left. The private described his reaction in a rare understatement. "It was very distasteful," he said.

The Pulitzer Prize-winning reporter stayed with the army until the Americans entered Paris. Then, weary and war-sick, he headed home for another rest. He hated to do it. "I feel like I'm running out," he said.

In January, 1945, Ernie Pyle was ready to go back to work again. The war in Europe was almost over and, although he would have liked to share the final victory with his GI friends, he realized that there would be far more to write about in the South Pacific.

Always nervous about getting killed in action, Ernie was now more cautious than ever. Much of his time was spent touring American bases and recreation areas behind the lines. Then one day he suddenly announced that he was going to cover a Marine invasion—"and the only way to do it honestly is to go with them."

Ernie joined a Leatherneck division that was landing on Okinawa, an island intended for use as a base for bombing Japan's big cities. But this particular detachment hit a soft sector of the island and he saw little action. He witnessed the rounding up of some Japanese prisoners and reported that his contribution to the capture consisted of "standing to one side and looking as mean as I could."

Ernie's next invasion experience was not so fortunate. The United States forces had decided to capture Ie Shima, a ten-mile-square island where the enemy had installed several crucial airstrips. It was an easy landing, but only because the island's defenders retreated into the hills.

Ernie went ashore on the second day after the landing, and a group of army officers invited him to make an inspection tour of the American emplacements. Although the Japanese were still hiding in the hills, it seemed like a safe journey. The men set out in a jeep, their easy chatter interrupted only by the occasional thud of mortar shells dropping on the open fields around them.

Suddenly the sharp clack-clack of an enemy machine gun echoed from behind a coral ridge in the distance. The men leaped out of the jeep and dove facedown into a ditch by the side of the road. When the sniper fire finally stopped, Ernie Pyle raised his head. "Are you all right?" he said to one of his companions.

In that instant, the machine gun clattered again. When it stopped this time, the officer turned to see if Ernie was all right. He spotted the reporter lying face up in the ditch. A bullet had struck him in the left temple. Someone called for a medic, but it didn't matter. The "little guy" had died instantly.

Although Ernie Pyle's body was later moved to the National Memorial Cemetery in Hawaii, a monument still stands on the side of the road in Ie Shima. It says:

> At This Spot
> The 77th Infantry Division
> Lost a Buddy
> ERNIE PYLE
> 18 April 1945

When the news of the tragedy was broadcast around the world, every infantryman in the United States Army knew that he, too, had lost a friend. President Harry S Truman summed up what they all felt when he said in a final tribute to Ernie Pyle, "No man in this war has so well told the story of the American fighting man as the American fighting men wanted it told. He deserves the gratitude of his countrymen."

10

Marguerite Higgins

On an August night in 1944, a twenty-five-year-old American girl sat at her desk in a Paris hotel room and jubilantly wrote in her diary: "I, war correspondent Marguerite Higgins, am a colleague of war correspondent Ernest Hemingway. How about that?"

When Maggie Higgins talked to the famous author or to any of the other reporters who made their headquarters at the Hotel Scribe, she pretended to be an old hand at covering wars. Actually, her olive drab correspondent's uniform was brand-new, and she was such a novice at foreign reporting that she wasn't even sure what the job involved.

Rather than take any chances, the petite blonde member of the *New York Herald Tribune*'s Paris bureau did everything she could think of. Before long the new "man" was filing stories like a veteran. Like every other correspondent in Paris, however, Maggie knew that the most exciting news in Europe was to be found, not in the newly liberated French capital, but several hundred miles to the east, where Allied troops were slowly pushing their way toward Berlin.

As the youngest member of the Paris bureau and a

woman besides, Maggie knew that her chances of getting to the front were slim. They improved when what Maggie liked to call "the Higgins Irish luck" began to work. Another reporter in the *Herald Tribune* office had wangled a place on an air force plane heading for the war zone. A few hours before he was supposed to take off, a crisis developed in the news office and he was forced to stay behind. He wondered if Maggie Higgins would like to take his place.

In a few minutes, Maggie had packed her musette bag, grabbed her typewriter, and checked out of her room at the Hotel Scribe. She left Paris in March, 1945. By the time she returned four months later, the war she had gone to cover was history and Maggie herself had joined the ranks of America's outstanding war correspondents.

Female war correspondents are few and far between. Several intrepid ladies had been in Cuba during the Spanish-American War, but until Maggie Higgins came along no woman reporter had ever gone into battle with an American army. Before she was through, the attractive blue-eyed Californian was at much at home in jeeps and foxholes as an army private, and the stories she sent home were good enough to win a Pultizer Prize.

Maggie Higgins's father had been an American aviator in World War I. He met her mother in France, married her after the Armistice, and took her off to Hong Kong where, in 1921, their only daughter was born. While Maggie was still quite young, the Higgins family moved to Oakland, California.

Fluent in two languages, Maggie, to the horror of her new playmates, spoke English with a French accent. When someone discovered that, on top of this failing, she had been born in Hong Kong, she was ridiculed for being a foreigner and taunted with nicknames like "Chinaman" and "Dirty Chink." Maggie soon learned to ignore the abuse. In the process she developed the self-assurance and toughness that would stand her in good stead as a newspaperwoman.

By the time Maggie Higgins graduated from the University of California in 1941, she had made up her mind to become a foreign correspondent. The first step, of course, was to land a job as a reporter. Maggie decided to work her way eastward from Oakland, stopping at every city along the way to apply for a job on the local paper. In a few weeks, Maggie, still jobless, had gotten all the way to New York.

On a hunch, the aspiring journalist took a subway to Times Square, walked up to a man who was selling newspapers on the corner of Broadway and Forty-second Street, and asked him where the offices of the nearest big paper were. The man pointed to the skyscraper on West Forty-first Street that was the home of the old *New York Herald Tribune*.

Maggie had already gotten too many brush-offs from receptionists in her travels across country. She decided not to risk another one. When she stepped off the elevator in the *Herald Tribune* offices, she bypassed the reception desk and joined a group of reporters who were heading into the city room. Once inside, she made her way across the huge office, introduced herself to the city editor, and told him she wanted a job.

There were no openings on the paper, but in those tense days shortly before Pearl Harbor more and more men were joining the armed forces. The way things were going, the editor told her, he might be grateful for any reporter—even a female one—before too long. "Come back and see me in a month," he growled.

It wasn't a job, but it was the closest Maggie had come to one in her transcontinental trek. She decided to stay in New

York and, while she waited for the *Herald Tribune* to find a place for her, enroll in Columbia University's Graduate School of Journalism. A few weeks after school opened, the *Herald Tribune* editor gave her a part-time job as a campus reporter. When she graduated, she became a permanent member of the staff.

Maggie Higgins had not forgotten her ambition to become a foreign correspondent. By the end of her first year as a city reporter, she had started a full-scale campaign to persuade the *Herald Tribune* to send her abroad. War had been declared the December after she entered Columbia, and she had a vague hope that she might see some of the fighting.

Maggie reminded the editors that she had already scored several impressive scoops, including an exclusive interview with an elusive union leader and another with China's first lady, Madame Chiang Kai-shek. She mentioned her fluency in French, hinting that it might come in handy if they wanted to send her to Paris. Both factors were in her favor. Still a third one tipped the scales. The vice-president of the *Herald Tribune,* Helen Rogers Reid, was eager to help another woman prove herself in the newspaper business.

In the summer of 1944, Maggie Higgins was appointed to the *Herald Tribune's* Paris bureau. Seven months later, thanks to "the Higgins Irish luck," she was on her way to war.

Her blonde curls stuffed under an army cap, her trim figure disguised by khaki fatigues, Maggie Higgins spent the last eight weeks of World War II following the American infantry as it marched into Germany. On at least one occasion, she managed to be ahead of the troops.

Maggie and the sergeant who had been assigned to accompany her drove into Dachau, the site of a large concentration camp. American forces were within striking distance of the town, and most of the citizens had already hung white flags on their doors to signal their surrender. Maggie and the sergeant decided it would be safe to drive out to the camp and see if they could get a story.

As they started up the long road that led to the camp's administration offices, they saw several guards waving white flags. The watchtowers around the compound, however, seemed to be manned by German officers. There was not a sign of a white flag in any of them.

The jeep ground to a halt in front of the main office and Maggie cautiously stepped out. Standing in the prison courtyard, she suddenly looked up. To her horror she saw that several rifles and a machine gun were pointing down from the watchtower directly in front of her. Behind the weapons she could see the sinister faces of almost two dozen SS men.

Maggie's first instinct was to turn and run, but she quickly realized that would be futile. Instead, she stared coolly up at the Germans and shouted, *"Kommen Sie hier, bitte. Wir sind Amerikaner.* (Come here, please. We are Americans.)"

The whole force—a total of twenty-two SS men—immediately clambered down from the watchtower and meekly handed over their guns to the war correspondent and her sergeant escort. The camp was officially liberated, and the overjoyed prisoners came bursting out of their barracks. They hugged and kissed Maggie and the sergeant, then hoisted them to their shoulders and paraded jubilantly around the camp. Maggie said later that, in her entire career as a war correspondent, the closest she came to physical injury was at the hands of the exuberant ex-inmates of Dachau.

Maggie Higgins's "capture" of the prison earned her an army campaign ribbon "for outstanding and conspicuous service with the armed forces under difficult and hazardous conditions." Her news report of the incident won her the New York Newspaperwomen's Club award as the Best Foreign Correspondent of 1945.

Ten days after Maggie's one-woman liberation of Dachau, the war in Europe was over. Maggie moved from the Paris to the Berlin office of the *Herald Tribune* and went on covering the news. She interviewed Adolf Hitler's butler, whom she found in hiding not far from the führer's lodge at Berchtesgaden: she shared a jeep with the captured chief of the German air force, Hermann Göring, and some months later covered the trials of the Nazi war criminals at Nuremberg.

Although Maggie Higgins had been a late arrival on the World War II scene, she was ahead of schedule for the next war. Early in June, 1950, she arrived in Japan to join the *Herald Tribune*'s Tokyo bureau. Three weeks later, when North Korean Communist forces invaded the Republic of Korea in the south, President Truman ordered United States forces into action. As soon as she heard the news, Maggie Higgins stuck a lipstick in her pocket, grabbed a notebook and typewriter, and took off on the first Korea-bound plane she could find.

Three days after the war began, Seoul, the capital of South Korea, fell to the enemy. Maggie, who had been in the city, was forced to retreat with its defenders. Her dispatches to the *Herald Tribune* told a disheartening story of an ill-prepared army completely overwhelmed by the superior forces of the enemy.

The United Nations voted to send a force into Korea, and on July 8 General Douglas MacArthur was selected to command it. Two weeks later, a cartoon appeared in a Russian newspaper captioned "MacArthur's First Victory." It showed the general running Maggie Higgins out of Korea at bayonet point.

Actually, it was not MacArthur, but Lieutenant General Walton H. Walker, commander of the Army Ground Forces, who objected to the presence of a woman in the war zone. He announced that Maggie was to leave at once. "This is just not the type of war where women ought to be running around the front lines," he said, completely overlooking the fact that she had already been covering the fighting for three weeks.

Although Maggie usually tried to conceal it, there was an Irish temper that went along with the Higgins Irish luck. It showed itself now. Maggie was infuriated, not because the order discriminated against her but because it jeopardized her newspaper's coverage of the war. When General Walker refused to rescind his command, Maggie hopped on a plane and flew to Tokyo to appeal directly to General Douglas MacArthur.

It so happened that Maggie and the general had been fellow passengers on the plane bound for Tokyo. Maggie had taken advantage of the coincidence to interview MacArthur. He had liked her story so much that he made her promise to get in touch with him if he could ever help her again. Maggie reminded him of the promise now. "I'm not working in Korea as a woman," she told him. "I'm there as a war correspondent."

Douglas MacArthur got on the phone to General Walker, and a few days later Maggie Higgins was back on duty. A cable from General MacArthur's Tokyo headquarters announced the good news to the *Herald Tribune* and added a word of praise for Maggie herself: "Ban on women correspondents in Korea has been lifted. Marguerite Higgins is held in highest professional esteem by everyone."

As soon as Maggie returned to Korea, she was ordered to appear in the headquarters of the commander of the Army Ground Forces. General Walker still thought the front was no place for a woman, he told her, but orders were orders. From now on, she was free to come and go as she pleased. "There's only one thing," he added. "The American public will never forgive me if anything happens to you, so please be careful and don't get yourself killed or captured."

Maggie did neither, but she endured practically every other hardship of that hard-fought war. She slept on tables and floors and anywhere else she could find room to curl up. She was frequently roused in the middle of the night to flee before advancing Communist forces. Almost as nerve-racking was the private war she fought against fleas. She once said that she cherished the gray tin of flea powder she had coaxed from an army medic almost as much as her typewriter.

In the early months of the Korean War, the United Nations forces took a terrific beating. Maggie wrote about it with total frankness. The war was going badly and she believed the American public ought to know about it.

When the Reds launched an offensive on the important harbor city of Pusan, Maggie took refuge in a regimental combat team headquarters some distance outside the town. The regimental commander was sure the flimsy building would be well out of range of the attack, but without warning a burst of machine gun fire tore through the cardboard-thin walls and ripped up the floorboards. It was followed by a hail of bullets spattering down from a hill directly behind the combat team's headquarters. Everyone in the building, including Maggie Higgins, hit the floor.

Maggie lay there certain that the entire building would soon be overrun and expecting any minute to find herself eyeball to eyeball with a North Korean soldier. As the barrage died down and none appeared, she scrambled to her feet. The casualties from the unexpected attack were extremely heavy, and Maggie joined a medical team that was frantically trying to save as many of the wounded as possible. Later, writing about the episode, she barely mentioned her own part in it. "One correspondent," she said modestly, "learned to administer blood plasma."

The story brought an immediate letter of criticism from a *Herald Tribune* reader. Colonel John H. Michaelis, the commander of the regimental combat team, wrote to say that Maggie Higgins had omitted several important details from her story.

"What she left out," he said, "was that, completely disregarding her own personal safety, she had voluntarily administered blood plasma to the wounded as they were carried into the temporary aid station. The aid station was subject to small arms fire throughout the attack.

"The Regimental Combat Team considers Miss Higgins's actions on that day as heroic, but even more important is the gratitude felt by members of this command toward the selfless devotion of Miss Higgins in saving the lives of many grievously wounded men."

Maggie was touched by Colonel Michaelis's gesture. "That Mike Michaelis should take time out to write that letter was deeply moving to me," she said. "I treasure that letter beyond anything that has happened to me in Korea or anywhere."

After weeks of fighting off Red offensives, General Mac-Arthur finally launched a counteroffensive—an amphibious landing at Inchon Harbor. Maggie Higgins was on hand for the surprise attack. She went in with one wave of United

States Marines, landed on the beach in a tangle of tanks, jeeps, and bulldozers, and was met by a barrage of shells, hand grenades, and bullets. Maggie ignored the danger and stayed on the beach until it was secured.

The Inchon landing paved the way for an eastward sweep across the Korean peninsula, and on September 26 the United Nations forces recaptured Seoul. When she was forced to retreat from the capital three months before, Maggie had vowed to return. Now she marched back right behind the United Nations army.

For correspondents, the Korean War proved to be one of the most dangerous wars in history. In the first month of fighting no fewer than five American reporters and photographers were killed. The surviving members of the press learned to be constantly on the alert. "Most correspondents carried arms of some kind," Maggie Higgins wrote. "The enemy had no qualms about shooting unarmed civilians. And the fighting line was so fluid that no place near the front lines was safe from sudden attack."

Already surrounded by danger, Maggie often went looking for more. GI Stanislaus Kovakopesky, pinned down in a foxhole, was astounded when a slender figure leaped in beside him and a feminine voice demanded, "How do you spell your name, soldier?"

On another occasion, Maggie wrote: "A reinforced American patrol accompanied by this correspondent this afternoon barreled eight miles deep through enemy territory. The jeep flew faster than the bullets which nicked just in back of our right rear tire."

By the middle of November, MacArthur's forces had pushed their way into North Korea, and the end of the war appeared to be in sight. Then, on November 26, the Chinese

Communists entered the war. Their first move was to launch a massive attack against the United Nations army in the Yalu valley.

The UN force was completely outnumbered. To make matters worse, it was fighting in temperatures that regularly hovered around fifteen degrees below zero. Nevertheless, Maggie Higgins hitched a ride in a C-47 and flew into the Yalu valley to report on the United States First Marine Division, which was bearing the brunt of the Chinese offensive.

"It was a battle all the way," she wrote. "The frost and wind howling through the narrow pass were almost as deadly as the enemy. Bumper to bumper, trucks, half-tracks and bulldozers slipped and scraped down the mountain. Half a dozen vehicles skidded and careened off the road. Mortars lobbed in and sometimes the convoy had to stop for hours while engineers filled in the holes. . . . Most of the Marines were so numb and exhausted that they didn't even bother to take cover at sporadic machine-gun and rifle fire. When someone was killed, they would wearily, matter-of-factly, pick up the body and throw it in the nearest truck."

Of the more than two hundred correspondents who eventually covered the Korean War, Maggie Higgins was the only woman. At first she attracted attention solely because of that fact, but she soon became better known for her energy and courage and, above all, the high standards of her work. In May, 1951, Marguerite Higgins was awarded journalism's most coveted honor, the Pulitzer Prize, for the excellence of her reporting in Korea. That same year, the Overseas Press Club gave her its George Polk Memorial Award "for courage, integrity and enterprise above and beyond the call of duty."

Maggie's bright blue eyes crinkled with delight when she

read still another tribute to her talents as a war correspondent. An editorial in the *Louisville Courier-Journal* declared: "Miss Higgins shows no desire to win a name as a woman who dares to write at the spot where men are fighting. Her ambition is to be recognized as a good reporter, sex undesignated. An envelope in our newspaper library's clipping file is labeled: Higgins, Marguerite—Newsman. We believe Miss Higgins would like that."

Miss Higgins did—very much.

When Maggie Higgins returned from Korea, she married an air force officer, Lieutenant General William Hall, and settled down to become a diplomatic reporter in Washington, D.C.

As the United States became progressively more involved in the war between North and South Vietnam, however, Maggie Higgins could not resist taking a closer look at the conflict. She was no stranger to Vietnam. Thirty years earlier, when she had contracted malaria as a child in Hong Kong, her parents had taken her to a mountain resort in central Vietnam to recuperate. Even more ironic, Maggie's grandfather, a French army officer, had died of a tropical fever contracted during a tour of duty in Indochina, as the French possession was then called.

Maggie Higgins made several trips to Southeast Asia, the last in 1965. She had been in Saigon only a short time when she developed a mysterious illness. At first the doctors thought it was malaria, but when none of the new "miracle" drugs could reduce the raging fever or alleviate the violent pain, they began to suspect it might be something worse. Maggie flew back to Washington and entered Walter Reed Hospital, but the doctors there were as baffled as the ones in Saigon had been.

Despite her almost constant suffering, Maggie insisted on

continuing the syndicated column she wrote for the Long Island paper, *Newsday*. Only when the mysterious malady had drained her of practically all her strength did she abandon her three-times-a-week schedule and write only one column that was published every Friday.

A team of specialists at Walter Reed Hospital finally diagnosed her illness as leishmaniasis—a rare tropical disease she had contracted in Vietnam. By then it was too late to save her. Maggie Higgins died in January, 1966, at the age of forty-five. A dedicated reporter to the end, she filed her last column right on schedule. It appeared in print the Friday before her death.

Index

INDEX

Dana, Charles, 33, 34
Dana, Indiana, 104
Davis, Mr. (father of Richard), 79, 80, 83, 86
Davis, Cecil (wife of Richard), 84, 86
Davis, Nora (sister of Richard), 81
Davis, Rebecca Harding (mother of Richard), 79, 83, 86
Davis, Richard Harding, 79-91
  background of, 79-80
  reports from Cuba, 81-82
  reports from Greece, 82
  reports on Spanish-American War, 83-84
  reports on Boer War, 84
  reports on Russo-Japanese War, 84-86
  in Mexico, 86
  reports on World War I, 87-90
Delane, John T., 1, 5, 10
Disraeli, Benjamin, 47, 48
Dublin, Ireland, 2, 3,
Dublin *Penny Journal*, 3

Earhart, Amelia, 107
Edward VII, king of England, 12-13
El Caney, Cuba, 72-74
England, 1, 5-10, 12, 25, 84, 93, 109
Eritrea, 101-102
Escourt, South Africa, 58-59
Ethiopia, 101-103

Fort Sumter, South Carolina, 11, 28
France, 21-25, 85, 113
Franco-Prussian War, 12, 21-25, 41, 85
Franklin, Massachusetts, 14
Frederick, Maryland, 18
Fredericksburg, Virginia, 28
Frémont, John, General, 16
French Legion of Honor, 101

George Polk Memorial Award, 126
Georgetown University, 92
Germany, 87-90, 93-96, 98, 105, 109, 119

Gibbons, Floyd, 92-103
  in Mexico, 93
  reports on World War I, 93-101
  wounded, 99-101
  awards to, 101
  in China, 101
  in Ethiopia, 101-103
  reports on Spanish Civil War, 103
Gibson, Charles Dana, 86
Göring, Hermann, 121
Goshen, Connecticut, 27
Grant, Ulysses S., 26-27, 31-32, 33, 34, 35, 36, 38, 39
Greece, 71, 82
Greeley, Horace, 30
Greene, Francis Vinton, 51

Haldane, Captain, 55, 59
Hall, William, General, 127
Hamilton, Ian, General, 58-59
Hardinge, Lord, 1
Harper's Monthly, 81
Harper's Weekly, 81
Hartzell, Oscar, Lieutenant, 98-100
Harvard Law School, 15
Havana, Cuba, 71
Hearst, William Randolph, 71, 74, 81-82, 91
Hemingway, Ernest, 116
Higgins, Mr. (father of Marguerite), 117, 127
Higgins, Mrs. (mother of Marguerite), 117, 127
Higgins, Marguerite, 116-128
  background of, 117-118
  reports on World War II, 116, 119-121
  awards to, 117, 121, 126
  reports on Korean War, 121-126
  in Vietnam, 127
Hitler, Adolf, 121
Hoar, George Frisbie, 15
Holland, 89
Hong Kong, 117, 127
Hooker, "Fighting Joe," General, 17-18
Hooker, Thad, 104-105

INDEX

Howard, John, 64
Howard, Roy, 107
Hull, Cordell, 108

Ie Shima, 114-115
Inchon Harbor, Korea, 124-125
India, 10, 53-56
Indiana University, 106
Ireland, 4
Italy, 101-102, 111
Ito, Admiral, 69-70

Japan, 67-71, 84-85, 101, 106, 121
Johns Hopkins University, 80
Johnson, Andrew, 21

Kaufmann, Konstantin, General, 43, 44, 45
Kelly, "Captain Jack," 2-3
Key West, Florida, 83
Khartoum, Sudan, 56
Khiva, 42, 44, 45-46, 50
Kinchow, Manchuria, 70
Kipling, Rudyard, 10, 84
Kitchener, Herbert, 56-58
Korea, 67-70, 121-126
Korean War, 121-126
Kovakopesky, Stanislaus, 125

Laconia (liner), 94-96
La Porte, Indiana, Herald, 106
Lee, Robert E., 16-18, 26-27, 31, 32, 35, 39
Lehigh University, 80
Leo XIII, Pope, 67
Liaoyang, China, 85
Lily Vale, Ireland, 2-3
Lincoln, Abraham, 11, 17, 19, 26-27, 30, 31, 34-35, 36-37, 38, 39
Litchfield, Connecticut, Enquirer, 38, 39
Liverpool, England, 96
Lockhart, William, 55-56, 59
London, England, 8, 13, 21, 22, 23, 24, 25, 46, 53, 55, 58, 82, 93, 109, 112
London Daily Graphic, 53
London Daily News, 47-48
London Daily Telegraph, 12, 54
London Morning Post, 52, 57, 58, 59, 63, 65
London Times, 1, 4, 5-6, 8, 10, 11, 12, 25, 82
Louisville Courier-Journal, 127
Louvain, Belgium, 89, 90
Lucan, General, 9

MacArthur, Douglas, 121-122, 124
MacGahan, Mr. (father of Januarius), 40-41
MacGahan, Januarius Aloysius, 40-51
background of, 40-41
reports Russian invasion of Khiva, 42-46
in Cuba, 46
in Spain, 46-47
reports on Russo-Turkish War, 48-50
injured, 48-49
Mad Mullah, 53-55
Maine, U.S.S., 71
Malakand Pass, India, 53-55, 56
Manchuria, 68, 70, 85
Manila, Philippines, 75
McClellan, George, General, 16-17
McLean, Wilmer, 39
Meerut, India, 55
Mejanel, 22-23, 24
Mexico, 86-87, 93
Michaelis, John H., Colonel, 124
Miller, Lee, 112
Miller, Webb, 101-102
Millet, Frank D., 49
Milwaukee, Wisconsin, 92
Minneapolis, Minnesota, 92
Mohammed Ahmed, 56
Montreal, Canada, 66, 78
Mount Kisco, New York, 87
Mussolini, Benito, 101-102

Napoleon III, emperor of France, 23

131

INDEX

New Lexington, Ohio, 40
Newsday, 128
New York, New York, 19, 20, 22,
   24, 25, 34, 40, 51, 69, 78, 79,
   80, 83, 102, 118
New York, U.S.S., 83
New York American, 78
New York Evening Sun, 80, 81
New York Herald, 40, 41, 48, 49,
   67, 82-83
New York Herald Tribune, 116, 117,
   118-119, 121, 122, 124
New York Journal, 71, 72, 74, 75-78,
   81-82, 91
New York Newspaperwomen's Club
   award, 121
New York Tribune, 15, 16, 19-20,
   21, 23-25, 27, 30, 31-32, 33-34,
   36, 37, 38, 39
New York World, 67, 68, 70-71, 82
Nicholas I, czar of Russia, 4
Nightingale, Florence, 8
Normandy invasion, 113
North Africa, 109-110
North Korea, 121, 125
North Vietnam, 127
Nuremberg trials, 121

Oakland, California, 117-118
Okinawa, 114
Oldham, England, 58, 64, 65
Omdurman, Sudan, 57
On the Great Highway (Creelman),
   66, 78
Overseas news bureau, 21

Palmerston, Lord, 10
Panama, 109
Panjkora, India, 55
Paris, France, 41, 89, 90, 96-97, 98,
   101, 113, 116, 119, 121
Pennefather, General, 6-7
Pershing, John J., General, 96-97
Philadelphia, Pennsylvania, 79, 81
Philadelphia Inquirer, 79
Philadelphia Press, 80
Philadelphia Record, 80

Philippines, 75
Philippopolis, Bulgaria, 48
Phillips, Wendell, 15, 20
Pioneer, 54
Pleven, Bulgaria, 49
Pope, John, General, 16
Port Arthur, China, 70
Portuguese East Africa, 62, 64
Powhatan, U.S.S., 40
Pretoria, Transvaal, 61-63
Prussia, 20-25, 41
Pulitzer Prize, 112, 117, 126
Pusan, Korea, 123
Pyle, Ernie, 104-115
   background of, 104-106
   reports on World War II, 109-
      110, 111-113, 114-115
   awards of, 112
Pyle, Mrs. Ernie (Jerry), 108, 109,
   111
Pyle, Marie (mother of Ernie), 105,
   106
Pyle, Will (father of Ernie), 104,
   105, 106
Pyongyang, Korea, 67-69

Raglan, Lord, 5-6, 8
Reid, Helen Rogers, 119
Reims, France, 89-90
Richmond, Virginia, 26-27, 31, 38,
   39
Roberts, Lord, 84
Robinson, John R., 47
Roosevelt, Theodore, 83
Russell, Mr. (grandfather of Wil-
   liam), 3
Russell, William Howard, 1-13, 14
   background of, 2-4
   reports on Crimean War, 1-2, 5-10
   first war correspondent, 2
   in India, 10
   reports on Civil War, 11-12
Russell, Mrs. William Howard
   (Mary Burrowes), 4, 5
Russia, 1, 4-5, 7, 8-10, 41-45, 48-
   50, 85
Russo-Japanese War, 84-86
Russo-Turkish War, 48-50, 51

132

INDEX

About the Author

Alice Fleming is a professional writer with a solid reputation in nonfiction for young readers. Among her numerous books are *Doctors in Petticoats, Great Woman Teachers,* and *The Senator from Maine: Margaret Chase Smith.* In addition to her weekly column in the *Boston Sunday Advertiser,* Mrs. Fleming regularly contributes articles to *McCall's, Ladies' Home Journal, House Beautiful,* and *Catholic Digest.* She and her husband, who also writes, live in New York City.